Essential
Kenya

by
MICHAEL LEECH

D1002986

PASSPORT BOOKS
a division of *NTC Publishing Group*
Lincolnwood, Illinois USA

Published by Passport Books, a division of NTC Publishing Group, 4255 West Touhy Avenue, Lincolnwood (Chicago), Illinois 60646–1975 U.S.A.

The contents of this publication are believed correct at the time of printing. Nevertheless, the publishers cannot accept responsibility for errors or omissions, nor for changes in details given. We are always grateful to readers who let us know of any errors or omissions they come across, and future printings will be updated accordingly.

Published by Passport Books in conjunction with The Automobile Association of Great Britain.

Written by Michael Leech
"Peace and Quiet" section by Paul Sterry

Library of Congress Catalog
Card Number 95–68322
ISBN 0–8442–8955–8

10 9 8 7 6 5 4 3 2 1

PRINTED IN TRENTO, ITALY

Front cover picture: Kilimanjaro

The weather chart displayed on **page 109** of this book is calibrated in °C and millimetres. For conversion to °F and inches simply use the following formula:

$$25 \cdot 4\text{mm} = 1 \text{ inch} \qquad \text{°F} = 1 \cdot 8 \text{ x °C} + 32$$

Contents

This book employs a simple rating system to help choose which places to visit:

✓	'top ten'

◆◆◆ do not miss
◆◆   see if you can
◆   worth seeing if you have time

Sporting traditional headdress: the Kikuyu tribe is Kenya's largest ethnic group

INTRODUCTION

Few parts of the world conjure up more natural wonders than Kenya. Here, in the wild, are all those animals you see on television and, increasingly, read about in the press.

For many decades it was a hunting preserve for gun-mad Europeans, eager to pot exotic beasts whose heads now gather dust on walls of historic halls. Fortunately, the fashion for killing wild animals has gradually been replaced over the past three decades, as people have realised there is just as much skill in shooting with a camera as with a gun. Animals, birds, insects and plants are now captured in the most amazingly lifelike images on film in Kenya, and death by gunshot is limited to poachers.

Your first visit to Kenya can be memorable and marvellous, for this is a seductive and beautiful country of many moods and climes. It is perhaps no longer the wonderfully wild place it was in the '50s, when vast herds of animals still grazed beyond the preserves, and the settlements had not burgeoned so far into the land. Kenya's principal problem is a fast growing population with a high birth rate, and many of its people moving into the towns, which have swelled from virtual villages to conurbations. Kenya's tribal and village life has transformed to a life of advancing sophistication and modernity in less than a century; and Nairobi has moved from being a frontier town to a busy, smart city – with stories of solar-topped hunters pursuing game down its main streets already folk-memories. Such writers as Karen Blixen, author of *Out of Africa*, give an intimate glimpse of the Kenya known by early European settlers.

East Africa appeared glamorous and unusual to the Europeans because of its commercial possibilities as an undeveloped area with a pleasant climate and a rich natural life. Even though Kenya is now much changed from those times, it is still vast and empty – despite its 23.5 million-plus population. Large parts of the country remain open and wild, and the scenery is immensely varied, ranging from tropical beaches to high, cool altitudes. (First reports of snow-covered mountains here, so close to the

Zebras in the great Rift Valley epitomise Kenya's natural attractions

INTRODUCTION

Mount Kenya is Africa's second tallest mountain; its weather-beaten peaks reflect a long history of erosion

Equator, were discarded by Victorians as being impossible!)

Kenya, unlike most other African countries, combines two major attractions for the visitor: superlative game viewing and a beach holiday beside the Indian Ocean. After the rigours (now comparatively smoothed away, with luxury often being a hallmark of the planned safari) of a visit to the famous game parks, you can swim and snorkel in the waters of the coastal beach resorts near Mombasa, joined by a remarkable railway to Nairobi; the journey is often tied into package trips, with recently updated de-luxe cars.

Kenya is also one of the most developed of all the emerging African nations, and there is a decided accent on human comforts. In Kenya you have a marvellous mixture of experiences: wildlife in abundance, and a sense of being in a decidedly different part of the world without being cocooned from reality. Hotels, while ranging from modern to budget, have a genuine feel of Africa, and the hospitality and courtesy of the Kenyan people is impressive. Their smiles and warmth contribute a great deal to the welcome of this remarkable and truly beautiful country.

BACKGROUND

The Place

Kenya is part of East Africa and this 224,959 square-mile (582,646 sq km) tract of land is roughly the same size and shape as France. Most of the country is arid, with only 20 per cent arable. But more than 4,000 square miles (10,000 sq km) are water, including Lake Turkana, the 3,000-square-mile (7,770 sq km) desert lake, and part of Lake Victoria. There are also numerous lakes along the central Rift, and large rivers, such as the Tana, the Athi, the Mara and the Turkwel.

Rising from the Indian Ocean to considerable heights, the country drops dramatically to a valley that slashes through almost the whole of Africa from north to south. This is the Rift Valley, and it provides Kenya with some of its most remarkable scenery and sights. It is as much as 50 miles (80km) across in Kenya and drops to 2,000 feet (600m) below the surface of the surrounding terrain. This enormous fault in the surface of the earth is studded with ancient and now extinct volcanoes.

The Valley is a grassland area, once filled with game, but now less so, due to population expansion. It is important in the history of the continent as a highway for the African peoples, and has always been home to the tall Masai. It is particularly rich in birdlife, and has several large lakes, which make unforgettable visits.

There are high ranges, dominated by Mount Kenya in the central area, the Aberdare Range in the Central Highlands, and the slopes of Kilimanjaro, the highest in Africa, peaking in neighbouring Tanzania to the south. The mountains were once volcanic (now dead or dormant) and they provide Kenya with its few areas of great fertility.

Kenya is bordered by the Indian Ocean for part of its eastern edge; here you find the beaches and resorts. Somalia occupies the rest of the eastern border, Ethiopia and the Sudan stretch from the north and Uganda is to the west. The whole southern border is occupied by Tanzania.

The People

Today's Kenyans seem to be descended from ancestors of the Bushmen, with incursions later by people from Ethiopia who herded stock and created farms. There is physical evidence of these Cushitic people in the Rift Valley and in the Highlands, in the form of stone cairns and some artefacts such as pottery and arrow heads.

The North of Kenya is the least developed and is largely arid, semi-desert with no large settlements. The people here are nomadic, the principal tribes being the Somali, the Turkana and the Samburu. This area is the least visited by travellers, and is not well known even by many Kenyans.

In the slash of the great Rift Valley are to be found the lean and elegant Masai, who are cattle herders. They have clung to a traditional way of life and their dress is unique. It is possible to visit their villages and watch tribal dances by young warriors made up with bizarre and elaborate hairstyles; but the Masai are, in fact, far from primitive: they are a wise and mature people and are well aware of the attraction of tourist money. Also cattle-based in the Rift Valley are the Kalenjin, though these peoples, the Nandi and the Kipsigi, are turning more to agriculture.

The Highlands, an area once kept as a preserve for European immigrants because of its excellent harvests of coffee, tea and pyrethrum (white flowers from which an insecticide is made), is the home-base of the Bantu-speaking Kikuyu, one of Kenya's biggest tribes. They are to be found in heavy concentration in Nairobi, and have tended to dominate government and business. Their main rivals are the Nilotic-speaking Luo, along the shores of Lake Victoria. This grouping is also widespread in present-day Kenya. The Abaluhya also live in this area, as do the Kisii, farmers of the higher levels. Although not a large tribe, the Kamba of the East were well-known to Europeans and Arab traders, for they are willing to travel, and were often employed as soldiers, guides and bearers. Originally cattle and livestock herders, they farmed the area, and their culture is a strong one, with

Surrounded by coastal forests, Gedi, now partially excavated, was once a wealthy centre of culture

considerable artistic expression in carvings, for example.

Islam dominates the whole of the coast area, which was the first part of Kenya to be explored. This is the land where Swahili comes from, and its people have been a mingling of disparate African origins for centuries. It is a cosmopolitan area, well known to early traders by sea, who founded bases here. Visitors to the resorts around Mombasa are in a good place to observe the Swahili cultures of this beautiful coastline, with its old settlements, intriguing ruins and mosques.

The Past

This is a land which bears the marks of immense and violent movements in eras long past. The Valley is important in studies of the earliest evidence of human origins. Volcanic action effectively sealed fossils of early life in layers that can be dated, and a visit to the National Museum in Nairobi (see page 19) will show several recent finds from excavations. Invasions started with descents from the north and the west, bringing new blood and new abilities, such as working with iron tools. There were also incursions along the coast where, from the mix of races, evolved the Swahili, the first traders of Kenya.

From the 1880s, Europeans were eager to slice up Africa into chunks 'belonging' to their respective nations. The two principal nations were Germany and Britain, with the former gaining Tanganyika (now Tanzania) and the latter Kenya and Uganda. During this time white settlers were encouraged, and although there were many genuinely honorable settlers, not much consideration was given to the local people. A whole series of restrictive land laws were promulgated and, as the land became increasingly taken up, Africans and Asians were banned from certain areas such as the Highlands.

World War I

Fast-changing social conditions were made even more complex with the advent of World War I, with both Germany and Britain in conflict. Kenyans saw at first hand the struggle in Tanganyika (German East Africa), and when the Germans lost the war, that part of Africa also came under British domination. The process of alienation of the local Kenyan population deepened. Political organizations began to flourish and gradually Africa began producing its own heroes, such as Harry Thuku of the Young Kikuyus and Jomo Kenyatta

Towards Independence

New waves of white immigration after World War II helped create more confrontation, and the growing nationalism of the Africans promoted a political party with the Kikuyu in ascendance. Then radical elements dedicated to overturning British rule formed underground cells, and from these roots sprang the Mau Mau. Conflict became inevitable; a State of Emergency was declared; and British troops came in to flush out the 'terrorists'.

Many Kenyans lost their lives, and although the movement was eventually put down, it had achieved its effect. Even white hard-liners began to see that there was no possibility of a white-dominated government in Kenya as then existed in Zimbabwe and South Africa.

Independence was very much in the air. A multi-racial Kenya was the answer, and in response to this the movement rolled on through the turbulent 1950s towards *Uhuru*: independence for Kenya. In 1963 elections confirmed the strength of the KANU party (Kenya African National Union), leading to the celebratory events of 12 December when Kenya became officially independent.

Independence

Uhuru caused an enormous upset in the country and many left, frightened at the prospect of a new black-dominated state under Jomo Kenyatta, Kenya's first Prime Minister. Kenya became a republic a year after its independence and Kenyatta became President at the head of the governing KANU party. He was much more of a careful conciliator than many expected, and certainly did not urge Europeans out of the country; rather, he kept many in administrative posts in his government.

Kenya has taken a long time to come close to the prosperity and standards dreamed of. A fragile economy was inherited, and there were many difficulties for the new nation, notably the vexed question of land reform. Much European-owned land was bought up and redistributed to make individual plots, and small holdings eventually began to make a contribution to the national economy.

Impala at dawn: an abiding emblem of East African wildlife

Industrialisation was needed, however, and growth was very slow at first. The Kikuyu-dominated government was a source of much grievance among other tribal groups, especially among their rival, Luo, who wanted a share in government. Accusations of corruption and nepotism, and the assassinations of popular leader Tom Mboya in 1969 and J M Kariuki in 1975, fuelled demands for change. But as he grew older and more entrenched Kenyatta increasingly assumed the appearance of a dictator, enjoying his reputation abroad as ally of the US and the UK. Kenyatta died in 1978, honoured in his country, yet departing under a cloud.

After Kenyatta

The years of *Harambee* ('Pull-Together') brought many changes and problems. The Luo

Picturesque palms are a major attraction for wildlife and visitors in Samburu National Reserve

had managed to attain some power, but minority groups seemed to go empty-handed. It was fortuitous that the next chief should come from a small tribe. Daniel Arap Moi is a Kalenjin, and he set about restoring confidence in the government with a number of popular moves against the prevailing corruption and restraints. He has pulled in closer ties with the West and improved relations with neighbours Ethiopia, Somalia and Tanzania, and managed to ride out the storms.

Kenya was for years a one-party state. Now it is multi party with KANU in command, though corruption has often raised an ugly profile. Moi inaugurated a policy called *Nyayo*, or 'steps of peace, love, unity' and he has so far remained in command, even though criticised for some of his actions or inactions. The country still faces many difficulties, although compared with the troubles experienced by most of the other African states, it has been very fortunate.

The Present

Kenya is divided into eight provinces, which are broken up into districts and divisions. The 1986 population figure was put at 21 million; now 23.5 it is expected to rise to 34 million by the end of the century. It has one of the highest population growths in Africa, and most of the people live on 30 per cent of the land, since so much of it is infertile. There is a high birth rate, but the death rate has dropped considerably in the last 25 years.

The visitor may see many examples of poverty and overcrowding, yet, compared with most African states, Kenya is very well off indeed. It is a country still rocked from time to time with violence and scandals; still prone to the occasional knock-out blows from nature, such as droughts and crop failures; still battling against new problems (the AIDS scare and reports of that modern plague being rife in Africa resulted in mass tourist defections, and tourism is Kenya's second biggest foreign income earner); yet, somehow, the country survives and retains its marvellous, almost hypnotic allure, for an appreciative throng of visitors from all over the world.

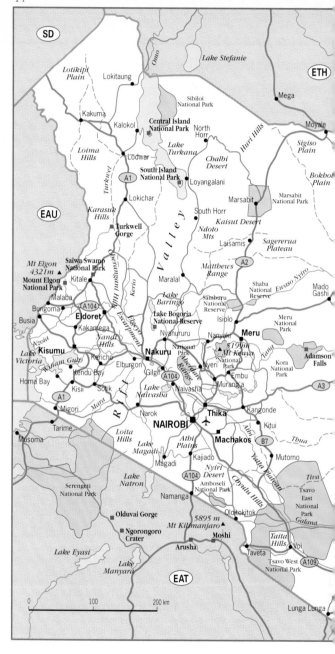

NAIROBI

Nairobi is a modern town in more ways than one: it is actually very new – barely 95 years old and from a station on the East African Railway 'Lunatic Line' from Mombasa to Lake Victoria: essentially a base for stores. There was no real planning in its initial siting; at this point the engineers had to pause to consider the problems ahead as the rail line ascended. From this unpromising, damp place, a small valley known in Swahili as *Ewaso Nairobi*, sprang a major city. It is a town that is thrusting and lively, and it has an exuberant but aggressive quality. Few travellers might be expected to seek it out, but it is, above all, a handy centre; almost anything

NAIROBI

can be bought there. Nairobi is an excellent base for seeing Kenya, and it is the centre of a web of communications.

The city has been pushed into the modern era at speed, and is now a place of contrasts, some quaint and some awful. It has a large floating population as more and more hopeful Kenyans arrive, forming a vast force of cheap labour. There is a lot of crime here, and you must take precautions, especially when going out after dark. A city with such contrasts of wealth and poverty is bound to have difficulties, and some Kenyans are very poor indeed.

Nairobi marks the meeting point of several areas of tribal lands, although the Kikuyu are its largest group of residents. The city has always numbered Europeans among its residents as well as Asians, many of whom arrived as railway workers and have stayed on to establish themselves as prominent citizens in leading professions.

The suburbs run the gamut of house design, from tin shacks in the truly decrepit and dangerous slums to replicas of European villas in the smart suburbs such as Muthaiga, a careful distance from the centre of town.

You may be surprised at the youth of this settlement, with the gleaming towers of its downtown section rising above the plain. Whatever its negative aspects (and there are more than a few) Nairobi is certainly a city of surprises.

The dramatic Nairobi skyline

Central Nairobi

Nairobi is fairly tight in layout, even if it is relatively unplanned. It is divided into a right-angled triangle, with the **Nairobi River** (such as it is) along one side, and, at the junction, the principle routes, **Haile Selassie Avenue** and **Uhuru Highway**. Not far away, on this southern side, is the main rail station at the foot of **Moi Avenue**, which goes straight up to the centre. The city centre is therefore fairly small and compact, although it is surrounded with great tracts of suburban development. If you need to penetrate these areas, check with your hotel as to the safety of travel in the relevant suburbs.

A walk along **City Hall Way** will show you the major monuments, most well set in spacious parkland. Within these gardens are several notable sights, such as the carefully guarded **Mausoleum of Mzee Jomo Kenyatta**; and not far off is an imposing bronze statue of the first President of the country, seated on a high plinth, and the neo-classical **Law Courts**. The large **Uhuru Park**, to one side, gives very good views of the government centre. It is a wide and attractive swatch of parkland, adding to Nairobi's reputation as a 'city of flowers', but should not be entered after dark.

To one side of the well-kept gardens of City Square is the busy **City Hall**, with its stone façade, and nearby, on the edge of Uhuru Park, is the Anglican **All Saints Cathedral**, looking as if it has strayed from an English country town, with its distinctive stone, gothic-style towers. The main avenues provide most of the interest, and the streets joining them are universally busy and lively. You will want to walk along **Kenyatta Avenue**, a very wide thoroughfare with malls down the middle and arcades running off it. Cutting a wide path along the southern border of the centre, **Uhuru Highway** acts as the principal traffic artery, pumping vehicles in and out of the city.

The Centre

The slice of streets between City Hall Way and Kenyatta Avenue, which are parallel, offers much to the browser and shopper, for here there are all sorts of small shops, galleries and good restaurants and snack bars. **Kimathi Street** has a notable gallery for African work, as well as a local landmark, the **New Stanley Hotel**, at the junction with Kenyatta Avenue. Here, at the outdoor **Thorn Tree Café**, you can sit and watch Nairobi hurry past, or check the central notice board for messages from friends. The tree itself was planted shortly after Independence, and rockets up even in this urban space.

The streets between City Hall Way and Kenyatta Avenue are the business heart of the town. **Mama Ngina Street** is particularly busy during the day: there are good African art showrooms and coffee places here. Parallel to it is **Kaunda Street** and **Standard Street**, which has a modern art shop and showroom in **Gallery Watatu** (there is another branch in the arcade beside the Six Eighty Hotel.

There is plenty to see along Kenyatta Avenue; one place not to miss is the interesting **Heritage Gallery**, which has a very large selection of curios and souvenirs. Other points on the avenue are the **British Council** offices, the **Post Office**, the **ICEA** office building (with great city views), **Nyayo House** and numerous shops and arcades.

Across the avenue the scene changes to a net of parallel streets heading up towards **University Way** and the museum district on its hill. These are crowded with humanity and circling cars desperately looking for a parking place. In the middle is the big concrete pile of the **City Market**, which makes a really interesting visit, whether you plan to buy or not. There is a large vegetable and fruit section, meat and fish departments and a big curio and basketwork area, where you may find more unusual souvenirs than the often spurious ones offered by street hawkers.

The market is on **Muindi Mbingu Street**, and behind it is an open market of souvenir stalls, spreading around and towards **Koinange Street**. There is also a good souvenir market before the brownstone classical **McMillan Library** on **Banda Street**.

Towards the junction of University Way and Uhuru Highway you will find the **French Cultural Centre** and **Goethe Institute**, which have regular cultural programmes.

Moi Avenue slants across the area to the right, and **Jevanjee Gardens**. (The Arboretum, State House Rd, is a collection of indigenous trees). A little further along Moi Avenue, beyond the main police station, is the renowned **Norfolk Hotel**, still a landmark and popular with locals, who gather every evening, and lunchtime too, at the famous terrace bar in front.

WHAT TO SEE

CATHEDRAL
City Hall Way

The Roman Catholic Cathedral of the Holy Family is very much a '50s structure, standing in green gardens and marked with a tall, narrow belltower. Its uncompromising interior, with great sheets of coloured glass, is austerely grand.

Open: most of the time.

♦♦
JAMIA MOSQUE
off Muindi Mbingu Street

This is a resplendent building of glittering domes and minarets, all set within spacious courtyards and landscaped grounds. It is simple, spacious and cool within, under its large dome, but non-Muslim visitors are not encouraged: a sign emphasises that this is a simple place of worship, with no 'touristic interest', and would-be visitors are directed towards officials. Nevertheless, you can go in after observing the usual formalities.

Open: most of the time, noting above restrictions.

The Kenyatta statue, Nairobi, commemorates Kenya's first leader

◆◆◆
KENYATTA INTERNATIONAL CONFERENCE CENTRE
City Square
Making its mark on the skyline, and most impressive, if not particularly beautiful, is the unmissable tower and 'high pie' of the Kenyatta International Conference Centre, which can be seen for miles and is a major part of the city's profile. The building is an unlikely combination of rural African and classical architectural styles. You can enter freely to look around, or ascend the tower for the view. The building is the headquarters of KANU, the ruling political party. The Centre, completed in 1972, is approachable from two sides.

There used to be a restaurant atop the landmark tower, 33 storeys high; now there is a viewing platform, and you can ascend free of charge. The police at the base may ask for a beer in response to a request, but they are very friendly and helpful, especially if you care to compliment the building.

This is a good place to see Nairobi, from its densely packed centre to the suburbs. The route to the airport can be picked out, as can the main road south towards Mombasa, and you can easily see the surrounding country on a clear day. You will gain an excellent sense of orientation here, and the tower is open most times, even quite late, except when the centre is being used. You can also ask to tour the centre itself, its conference hall being well equipped and one of the largest in the world.

Open: every day, except when there are major meetings.

◆◆◆
THE NATIONAL MUSEUM ✓

off Uhuru Highway, on Museum Hill Road
If you enjoy birdlife as well as the fantastic animals of East Africa, then the rich variety of this part of the world is a joy. But it has to be said that a visit to the National Museum makes a very good prelude to any kind of safari or bird trip into the country.

Although stuffed animals and birds are not the only thing to be seen in this remarkable collection, which is one of the most important sights of Kenya, they make up quite a big section.

The animals are set in

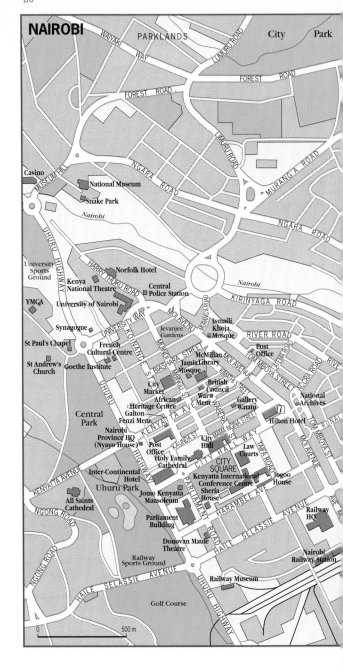

Kariokor
Market

KARIOKOR

MUTHURWA

atmospheric dioramas and are life-size (except for the elephant), which makes the Giant Eland, for example, appear truly enormous in its shadowy glade. These are dramatically presented exhibits, but the birds are merely stuck in prosaic cases and there is no attempt to give a suggestion of their background. Still, they can be studied in close-up, and the colours and forms are often extraordinarily beautiful.

Seeing them here, stuffed or pictured, makes one long to view them in the wild, and you will learn a lot, even if ornithology is not your greatest passion.

The Hall of Palaeontology should not be missed; in addition to the traces of our human forebears it also has creatively displayed dioramas of the imagined life of early man and the other primitives.

In neighbouring Tanzania, Mary Leakey and her husband Louis uncovered many extraordinary examples of early life. (Their son, Richard, has directed the National Museum, and held conservation posts in government). The large reproductions of rock paintings are Tanzanian, as are the intriguingly ancient pairs of footprints made in mud by early human ancestors: (two adults, one with smaller feet walking in the footsteps of the other, and a child).

The museum also has a section devoted to Kenya's recent history, with a parade of photographs leading up to the declaration of independence,

NAIROBI

Steam along to see the treasures of the Railway Museum

and there are also presentations of the folk culture of the country with original examples of the many strands of tribal culture.

Although outside the main hub, the Museum is easily reached from central points either by walking (about half an hour) or by taxi or bus. Allow a little time to look at the museum's shop, which has some first-class examples of folk art.
Open: daily 09.30–18.00hrs. Admission charge (Kenyans and students get special admission rates).

◆◆
RAILWAY MUSEUM
to the left from the station; well-indicated
This sprawling site has a plethora of items that offer a potted history of Nairobi as well as being of interest themselves. Nairobi grew out of a railway shunting yard and depot for the railway builders, and you will notice first the collection of rusting but still impressive old locomotives, parked rather forlornly outside the building.

Closer inspection reveals that you can climb into the cabs, and touch and play with old driving aids. One in particular is always drawing notice: the number 12 coach, from which a traveller, Charles Ryall, was dragged and eaten by a lion. The main building has a chaotic yet genuinely fascinating collection of visual material, old photographs and drawings of the early line, so important to the country's development. Photographs of old stations and engines can be found in the museum's annexe.
Open: every day, 8.30–16.45hrs; closed Saturday afternoons. Admission charge.

> Information on opening times, etc has been provided for guidance only. We have tried to ensure accuracy, but things do change and we would advise readers to check locally before planning visits to avoid any possible disappointment.

Accommodation
The city has a fair variety of hotels, although not a great number, and lower priced ones tend to be in the suburbs, which are not always easy, or even

safe, to get to late at night. Unless you are on a really tight budget, or want to stay where the people live, you would be wise to stay in the centre even if it costs more.

In the top luxury class there is the city centre **Hilton** on Watalii Street (tel: 334000), with terrace garden and pool, or the **Inter-Continental**, City Hall Way (tel: 335550), in a good location facing the park. Old-timers will still wax nostalgic about the **Norfolk Hotel** (tel: 335422), an Edwardian building on Harry Thuku Road, almost as old as the city, recently refurbished and just outside the centre. It has gardens and a sociable air on its famous front terrace.

Nairobi Serena, Nyerere Road and Kenyatta Avenue (tel: 725111) is central; and also in the middle of town is the older but still very acceptable **New Stanley Hotel**, Kenyatta Avenue and Kimathi Street (tel: 333233), with its pleasant open air Thorn Tree Café, a local landmark.

Quality hotels:

Hotel Ambassadeur, Moi Avenue (tel: 336802), a large modern hotel; or slightly away from the centre, in the pleasant Museum district, the **Boulevard**, Harry Thuku Road, (tel: 227567), with gardens and a pool and probably quieter than most. Outside the centre is the **Jacaranda Hotel**, Chiromo Road (tel: 445817); the **Panafric Hotel**, Kenyatta Avenue (tel: 720822); or perhaps try the **Windsor Country Club**, Ruaraka (tel: 217479).

Bargain hotels:

The very reasonable **Fairview** on Bishops Road (tel: 723211), or the self-catering kitchen-equipped **Heron Court Apartment Hotel** on Milimani Road (tel: 720740). A bargain, and right in the centre, with a friendly first floor bar, is the **Six Eighty Hotel**, Muindi Mbingu Street and Kenyatta Avenue (tel: 228177). The **Central YMCA Hotel** is at State House Road (tel: 728825) and there are other branches at the Shauri Mayo Hostel, Ambira Road (tel: 558383) and in Nairobi South, on Muhoho Avenue (tel: 504296). The **YWCA** is at Nyerere Rd (tel: 724789). For details of **Kenya Youth Hostels** (tel: 721765).

Restaurants

The city has no lack of eating places, although to find African food you will have to search hard. Fresh seafood is good in Kenya, and it is best eaten simply or Indian- or Oriental-style. There are plenty of Chinese, Indian, Italian and Thai places, and many Nairobi restaurants have entertainment in the evenings. There are also numerous good snack bars in the centre, usually only open until late afternoon.

Top ranking places include **Carnivore** (tel: 501775), out on the Langata Road, where you have steaks and grilled game and dancing on weekends. Out at the Casino, the new **Galleria** gives a grand view from its picture windows and is very smart.

For Kenyan food in a simple setting, try the restaurant at the **Heritage Gallery** on Kenyatta

Avenue, where a special buffet is available on Fridays (entry Banda Street).

Hotel food is international in style: try the **Terrace Café** at the New Stanley Hotel. Best of all, and a bargain (day times only) is the very popular **Jax**, in the Old Mutual Building on Kimathi Street. In the market district, the **Blue Kat**, Muindi Mbingu Street (tel: 229418), is popular.

There are plenty of vegetarian restaurants and on the street fruits of all kinds are always on offer, along with roasted maize ears, while in the suburbs there are numerous fish and chip shops.

The **Safeer** (tel: 227567), at the Hotel Ambassadeur, presents Indian Mughal food. **Tamarind** (tel: 338959) is good for seafood. **Supreme** is a budget Indian restaurant on Tom Mboya Street, well recommended. **Trattoria**, at Town House on Kaunda Street, is locally popular.

Shopping

Arts and crafts can be bought at the local markets, with a concentration at the main **City Market**, nearby **Banda Street**, outside the Library, or, best of all, the galleries, such as the **Heritage Gallery**, or others, in the ground floor of the old Mutual Building or on Mama Ngina Street. Here items will be more costly but guaranteed not to be turned out by the dozen. There is good basketwork at the market (compare prices), with coloured patterns and sometimes beadwork, and there is an artisans' market at **Kariokor** which is very popular. It is accepted, indeed often expected, to bargain at the markets and stalls.

There are shops in the museums of Kenya, often well worth checking out for reasonable prices; and you are more likely to find genuine artists' works here.

For the top quality arts and crafts of the country (not from all over Africa) try the **Gallery Watatu**. There are two branches: one at Standard Street on the first floor, and one in a mall behind the Six Eighty Hotel. Browsers are made welcome, and some of the articles on offer are spectacular and original, including paintings, drawings, hangings, sculpture, batiks and collages.

There are other galleries on **Standard Street**, with a mixture of arts and crafts, mostly commercial. In the arcades, Indian shops sell fabrics and clothing.

For local supplies there are good supermarkets in the city, but they are often crowded, and you may have to wait at the check-out counters if it happens to be pay-day.

Ethnic crafts at Nairobi Market

NAIROBI SUBURBS

The Athi Plains, once a spacious place for a great concentration of game animals, surround the capital. Home for most of Nairobi's million or more inhabitants, the suburbs encroach on these spaces, with wealthy developments to the north, and poorer houses clustered to east and south.

In Nairobi you can still see some of the original corrugated iron buildings that made up the early central section, hiding behind cluttered shops – but not many, for Nairobi is in the middle of a building boom, and more noticeable from the suburbs are the many modern tower blocks. Corrugated iron shacks are still common in the poorer suburbs, however, although new brick and concrete houses are being built for sale as speculation – often beyond the reach of the purse of the average citizen.

On the edge of the suburbs, near the airport, is the city's own national park, where lions still roam and can often be heard. At

Close encounter of the natural kind at the Giraffe Centre

night, particularly, you can still feel close to the primeval Africa that existed less than a century ago, now buried under the accretions of suburban wood and concrete.

Neat but expensive rows of new brick houses press up against the borders of the park: this is a city growing and spreading very fast.

It is easy to take a tour to the affluent suburbs to the west, divided by ancient forest land and carefully fenced paddocks for horses, and some distance from the centre. Many resemble well-off suburbs in Europe and the US, with large houses and gardens.

In the closer suburbs there are almost no tourist attractions, and you will need to take a taxi or a *matatu* (converted van) if on a budget (but these can become very overcrowded and are better as an adventure than as a regular form of transport (see **Directory** under **Public Transport**, pages 122–123).

NAIROBI SUBURBS

WHAT TO SEE

◆◆
THE *BOMAS* OF KENYA

*a mile (2km) from the main
gate of the National Park
towards Langata*

This is a long-established
attraction: an attempt to focus on
the folk past of the country using
buildings (the *bomas* are
traditional homesteads) and
dance. Professional dancers
show you a range of supposedly
authentic tribal dance, and an
interesting mêlée it is. The show
lasts about two hours in a wide
ampitheatre, and is very
popular with local groups on
weekends, when it can become
quite crowded and lively –
perhaps the best time to go! At
these times there is also a disco,
so you can combine culture with
fun. The *bomas* are beyond the
entrance to the National Park; if
travelling by bus you can ask to
be dropped off here.
Inevitably there are souvenir
stands too, and the admission
charge includes the show. It is
perhaps more commercial than

it needs to be, and the dances
are all presented by the same
troupe of performers, but some
of the selections are both
dramatic and thrilling, and it
does give an insight into the
variety of dance in just one
country of East Africa.
Open: every day; dances
presented at 14.30 or 15.30hrs.
Regular bus departures from
Nairobi bus terminal.

◆◆
GIRAFFE CENTRE

Langata

This popular attraction is run by
Daphne Sheldrick, and, if you
have children, an absolute must.
They can climb a little tower,
meet the giraffes face to face
and feed them pellets of special
food. The animals' big rough
tongues sweep up the food to
squeals of delight from the
children. There are usually five
giraffes in residence, and a
small museum offers displays
about these curious creatures.
Open: every day.

The Karen Blixen Museum

◆◆◆ KAREN BLIXEN MUSEUM ✓

Karen House, near the main crossroads at Karen Dukas, nine miles (15km) south of Nairobi

Turn left through paddocks, with horses and fine views of the hills, towards the museum on Karen Road, which can be a bit rough in parts. The house, which belonged to writer Karen Blixen, who recorded her life here in the classic book *Out of Africa*, is a low-slung building with a red tiled roof and urns on the top.

There is not much to see here but there is a definite atmosphere of the old days in the plain, well polished rooms, curtained with lace and sparsely furnished; and even an antique telephone. Outside, the millwheels around which Karen Blixen's guests the Masai sat to talk to her can still be seen. It is a very pretty place with its views of the Ngong Hills which Blixen loved so much, and the shop here is well worth visiting for souvenirs of better quality than usual. Note the tall coffee bush outside the front door; you can buy the local coffee beans, though they are expensive. The house was built in 1912 and the Blixens moved in five years later; Karen Blixen left when the farm failed in the '20s.

This small and elegant little house has been given a glamorous mystique by the film *Out of Africa* in which the oddly chosen talents of Meryl Streep and Robert Redford combined to make a big box office hit. Inevitably, the bringing of the name of Karen Blixen (whose pen name was Izaak Dinesen) into the wide world of filmgoers has brought a lot of interest to her one-time farm, and since it figured in the film it has become familiar to many. Shorn of the coffee plantation it was once centered on, the stone house stands in a sweep of sun-gilded garden and still manages to give a sense of what it was like when the novelist lived there as a working farmer. A tour will take you out from central Nairobi; it is also possible to take a round trip by taxi.

Open: every day 09.30 to 17.30hrs. Admission charge.

◆◆◆ NAIROBI NATIONAL PARK ✓

main entrance on the Langata road, about eight miles (13km) from city centre

Even if you have only a short time and no days allotted to visiting one of the major Kenyan parks, you should save an afternoon for a visit here. It is virtually in the suburbs and easy to reach. One of its major aspects is its educational role, and children have a wonderful live lesson before them in this small 44-square-mile (114 sq km) reserve, where a surprising variety of wildlife can be seen.

Nairobi schoolchildren are taken through the very good Wildlife Education Centre, gaining as they go a sense of

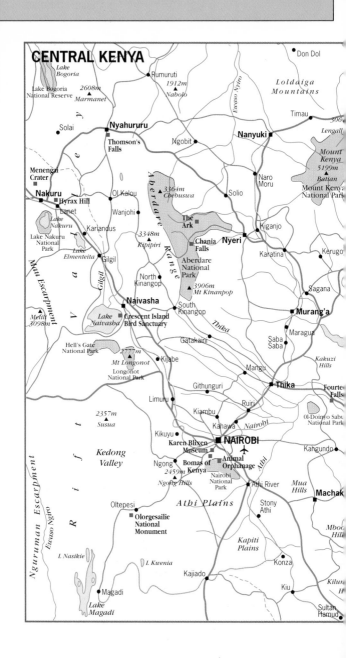

the importance of conservation, not just for altruistic reasons but because the African wildlife is a vital tourist resource.

You can spend a day at the park and still not see all of it. It may not look large on a map, but inside the boundaries there is plenty to view, from buffalo to baboons; lions are fairly common, and the elephant is one of the few species of large beast not represented.

The animals are not confined within the park, for the zone is unfenced (only certain spaces are being fenced in East Africa to preserve endangered animals – particularly the rhinoceros – from the danger of poachers).

Animals move in and out of the park from the plains beyond, through the Kitengela 'corridor', and provide a constant seasonal change. (Numbers tend to increase before the rains of the autumn months.) While the rhino is rare in all parks now, this is one place you are almost sure to see this extraordinary and intriguing creature.

The best times to visit are very early, or late afternoon for viewing. Take a good pair of binoculars and you may even be lucky enough to spot a leopard. Allow plenty of time and drive slowly, stopping frequently. (You cannot get out except at designated picnic spots, and even these are at your own risk, although you should be safe enough if you observe precautions.)

The park has a remarkable range of scenery and it seems to be quite easy to get around, but don't assume you can quickly drive back: allow lots of time for transporting yourself along the often very rough tracks, and remember that on weekends the park can get crowded; it is very popular with local people. If you are waiting for sunset, when the lions stretch and move out of the shade for nocturnal activities, remember that the main gate is closed at 19.00hrs. There are other exits, so you will be able to leave, although maybe less conveniently.

You can take a tour to the park from the city; your driver should be knowledgeable, or you can hire a professional guide. A good deal of information is passed from car to car, and in this way you are likely to see many more of the various beasts.

Other gates can be found along the Mombasa Road; pick up a plan at the entrance.

Open: all year, during daylight

Left holding the baby, a male ostrich stands guard over eggs

hours from dawn to sundown. Fee per vehicle.

Regular hourly bus service from Nairobi centre.

NGONG ROAD FOREST
off the Ngong Road from Nairobi

Just before Karen and its shopping centre (Karen Dukas) you pass through a pocket of the ancient woodland that once carpeted the area. This is the Ngong Road Forest, and it gives you a fragmentary idea of how the country must have looked and sounded (it's filled with bird calls) to early arrivals. Aside from the eucalyptus trees, most of the forest is natural and of native growth.

WORLD WIDE FUND FOR NATURE ANIMAL ORPHANAGE
Langata Gate of the National Park

Here is a rather pathetic show of orphaned animals, a collection of creatures that have been abandoned or found sick in other parts of the country. If you have children they may well want to stop here and wait for feeding time, in which they can take part.

The World Wide Fund for Nature hopes that by creating this orphanage it can re-introduce the healthy animals to the wild; but some seem to be permanent residents.

Open: same times as National Park, but closes promptly at 17.30hrs.

EXCURSIONS FROM NAIROBI

The Aberdare Highlands, a stark volcanic massif edged by forests

You will find a variety of scenery and attractions around the capital, most within easy reach on moderately good roads, some on the rail line. Most attractions are to the north and west.

♦♦♦
ABERDARE RANGE (ABERDARE NATIONAL PARK) ✓

six miles (10km) west of Nyeri
The Aberdare Range (known to the Kikuyu as *Nyandarua* or Drying Hide, from its skyline) is one of the wild areas least touched by humanity; here the deep rainforest is mostly intact. Less farmed than the area round Mount Kenya, this heavily wooded and mountainous region was made a National Park in 1950. Rare creatures found here include melanistic cats – serval, leopard and genet. The Aberdare Range backs onto the great gash of the Rift Valley,

and has several well-known attractions.

Treetops (tel: Nyeri 2424) is the famous game-lodge in the Aberdare Range that gained immediate and world-wide notice when a young Princess Elizabeth, on a visit to Kenya in 1952, heard of her father's death and her accession to the British throne. The place has gone through many vicissitudes since then, having been burned down and then moved, and is not recommended as much as it used to be: it is not far from the edge of the park, and civilisation is creeping near.

There is also a vegetation problem, but on overnight stays you should still see animals such as buffalo and elephant. To stay here you have to book a package tour from **Block Hotels** in Nairobi (tel: 335807) or an agent, starting from the Outspan Hotel near by

EXCURSIONS FROM NAIROBI

Tucking in: the speckled mousebird

(children under seven not admitted).

The nearby **Mountain Lodge** is open to the public (ATH group). More interesting than Treetops is **The Ark**, an equally eccentric lodge, also in the same park, beyond the Treetops Salient, that extends eastwards towards Nyeri. It is further in and placed in an area still heavily wooded, where there is more game than elsewhere – that is if its one-time guardian R J Prickett is to be believed in his very readable book, *The African Ark*, although this was written in the early '70s.

The Ark is 20 years old now, yet a big attraction to anyone visiting the Aberdare Range, where leopards are still seen and, occasionally, the rare and elusive woodland antelope, the bongo, emerges shyly from the forest to use the salt-licks. There is also a vast variety of birds in the flowering bush growing around the lodge and its pool.

There is a buzzer system for special visits of rare creatures, and many people sit up all night hoping to catch sight of unusual beasts. An underground hide, as at Salt Lick, allows you to 'go below' to watch animals at very close quarters, and there is also a tree walk over the scrub. The visit should be at least overnight and maybe longer.

Book through **Lonrho Hotels** (Central Reservations tel: 221047), in Nairobi; the trip leaves from the Aberdare Country Club at Mweiga (tel: 55620 in Nairobi), using the Ark Gate to climb to the pool that is known as the Waterhole of the Leeches. Children under seven are not admitted to the Ark.

The Aberdare Range might be called a vertical park, for there are various flora at the different levels; thick woodland around The Ark gives way further up to dense growths of bamboo and eventual bare moorland on the upper and distinctly chillier slopes.

This is a place for the botanist and gardener, as well as the animal lover, and shrubs and plants are as prevalent as ever, unlike the less fortunate plundered animals.

◆ EMBU

junction of Kitui and Nairobi roads to Meru

Capital of the Eastern Province, this small town is set along the base of a hill offering places to stay and providing a handy base for climbing Mount Kenya (try nearby **Chogoria** for the east side).

◆◆ HELL'S GATE NATIONAL PARK

south of Lake Naivasha on a rough path towards the Narok Road

This is a good scenic walk, although a long and tiring one, which can be made using Naivasha as a base. A marked track takes you to **Fischer's Tower**, a column of volcanic rock; at the other end is **Ol Basta**, a similar rock formation. The **Gorge** is impressive, with lots of animals and birds to see, and there is a viewpoint from the top of the ravine at **Olkaria**, site of a thermal station. Accommodation is limited to camping and you should take a picnic and plenty of bottled water.

Nearby, in the **Longonot National Park**, is the once volcanic **Mount Longonot**, which can be climbed by the energetic from the village of the same name. You can go down to the crater floor or walk around the encircling path. Wear good shoes or boots, and allow lots of time for the exploration and stiff climb, which will reward you with a marvellous view of the Rift Valley.

Open: all year. Admission charge.

◆◆ MACHAKOS

southeast of Nairobi, off the main Mombasa road

An unusual, friendly town, home of the Akamba people. You will find this a good (and little visited) place to buy unusual and colourful baskets. There is a large open-air **market** and an impressive **mosque**. From Machakos a road goes through attractive scenery to **Kitui**, where Pastor Krapf, a German missionary, set off to become the first European to view Mount Kenya. (There is a memorial to him at Mombasa.)

◆◆ MERU

on the new road north from Nairobi, through Embu

An interesting straggle of a town, with a large **market** and a **museum**. Set on a hillside with sweeping views. Mainly used as a base for exploring the nearby national park (see below).

◆◆◆ MERU NATIONAL PARK

about 22 miles (35km) east of Meru; follow route east for Maua then signs

Meru was the site of George and Joy Adamson's adventure with lions which was related in Joy Adamson's book *Born Free*, and which brought fame to Kenya. It is still very difficult to get to even though relatively close to Nairobi by road; consequently there are concentrations of animals, rather than of vehicles. Even so these are not easy to see, for Meru is a park with rich vegetation and an atmosphere all its own.

Meru has lodges with viewing terraces, as at **Mulika Lodge**, managed by KTDC, (tel: 20000), and campsites. The Tana River, along the southern edge of the park, marks the border with one of the neighbouring four reserves, Adamson's Kora, which, like the others, is mostly rough scrub and not easy to visit. The meeting of the Tana with the Rojewero, a long wriggle of a river running down from Mulika through the park, is marked with dramatic cliffs recently named **Adamson's Falls**. Many people choose to camp out here (admission charge, plus an extra fee per car).

Open: all year.

Towering over the forests, Mount Kenya is sacred to the Kikuyu

♦♦♦
MOUNT KENYA NATIONAL PARK

Central to the area is the imposing bulk of Mount Kenya, the second highest mountain in Africa, rising to 17,058 feet (5,199m) at its tallest peak, Batian. There are two others, Nelion and Lenana, making up the massive mountain, with its circumference of more than 250 miles (402km). Like the Aberdare Range, this splendid mass is volcanic in origin and was made famous in 19th-century Europe with the much questioned report of snow on its peaks.

Surrounded by farmland and prairie, the mountain is a National Park from the 10,500-foot (3,200m) contour, and here you can climb up Lenana in quiet and cold solitude to gain a view. (Remember that even

though it is the lowest of the three 'horns', it is very high, and by no means an easy climb. The altitude needs getting used to, so if you want to trek up the mountain you must be healthy and allow several days. *You cannot go on your own.* Check on the supplies you will need, and make sure you have warm clothes and protection against the wet in the high altitudes. You will either be camping or staying very cheaply at basic mountain huts, so a bed-roll is also a necessity.)

You can also walk on the open moorland (after gaining permission, or as a member of a group) and there is plenty of fishing in the streams, which have been stocked with trout. (Fishing equipment can be hired locally.) Unusual, and surprising against the snow-spattered peaks, are the curious Afro-Alpines, the giant lobelias, groundsels and heathers growing above bamboo thickets on rough, stony moorland high up towards the summits. Mount Kenya is a sacred place to the local Kikuyu, whose settlements and farms now surround the mountain, and it is the home of their god, credited with holding the 'mysterious whiteness'.

MUKURUENE

Not far from Murang'a (see below) is a site revered by the Kikuyu, their 'garden of Eden', where the ancestors of the nine tribes were created in their mythology. Mukuruene wa Nya-Gathanga is a simple spot, and the fig-tree under which Gikuyu and Mumbi, the founders, made sacrifice and bore their nine daughters, is a replacement.

MURANG'A

on the road to Nairobi from Embu

A quiet, small town, which is particularly important for being the centre of the Kikuyu

Homeland. Murang'a, once known as Fork Hall and a Kikuyu reserve, has a church founded by the Archbishop of Canterbury in 1955 as a memorial to the many Kikuyu who died in Mau Mau killings. Within the **Church of St James and all Martyrs** is a mural by Chagga artist, Elimo Njau, depicting a black Nativity, a Last Supper and a Crucifixion, all in recognizably local African settings.

NAIVASHA

main road northwest from Nairobi; accessible by rail

Naivasha is approached from Nairobi by the well-metalled Uplands Road. It enters the Rift and offers panoramic views as it slips down towards the town and the fresh-water Naivasha Lake, a major attraction with a pleasing climate. You can stop at the town (a fairly ordinary place, but useful for buying supplies for a stay at the lake), before going on to visit the shore. Consider a boat tour to see lake birds,

Roadside shops feast the eye

gazelles and waterbuck (be wary of them) on the narrow slip of Crescent Island. You are usually taken here on the regular boat run, and can then spend as much time there as you wish. This attractive lake can get quite churned up in bouts of bad weather.
Boat trip: from the Lake Naivasha Hotel, charge.

◆
NANYUKI
junction of main north road from Nairobi
Set right on the Equator, this is a neat, small town with major military bases. There are plenty of shops, wide streets, and an agreeable country air. It was once the centre of vast game herds (ranching the wild animals, such as rhino, is now being practised, as in South Africa).
Nanyuki shops sell well-designed hand woven articles, which can be seen at the spinners' and weavers' workshops; there are also attractive, old-fashioned shops such as the Settlers' Store.

◆
NGONG HILLS
beyond the road to Ngong from Nairobi
There are wonderful views from these knobby hills, with their distinctive skyline, west of Karen. A path along the top provides a memorable walk with spreading views, and you may well see buffalo and antelope – but, also unfortunately thieves. It may be advisable to enquire about a guide from the Ngong police.

NYAHURURU
along a new road from Nyeri
Nyahururu is on the Equator, and the town is famous as the site of Thomson's Falls (once the name of the place). It is a market centre, and is still something of a frontier town, with connections onwards to the north. The falls themselves are on the edge of town and very popular, although there are other and more beautiful watercourses such as Chania Falls in the Aberdare Range. But this one is easy to get to, and has viewing points.

◆
NYERI
approach by major roads between Mount Kenya and Aberdare Range
A sizeable business centre with busy markets and a lot going on. Nyeri calls itself capital of Kikuyuland. It has a delightful climate, lots of shops and is surrounded by small *shambas*, all growing fruit and vegetables in great profusion in its fertile soil. There are also tea, coffee and macadamia nut plantations. A good centre for explorations of the nearby Aberdare mountains.

OLORGESAILIE
towards Magadi from Nairobi
Olorgesailie is a prehistoric site: half a million years ago it was a settlement of lake-people. It is now listed as a tiny National Monument. Here, in this stark, forbidding valley, is a primeval lake, long dried up and deeply eroded, which the Leakeys explored, excavating tools and

*Thomson's Falls, 237 feet (72m),
skirts the Marmanet Forest*

fossilised bones, now displayed
in the open. There is a small
museum.

Also to be seen, a short distance
to the south, is **Lake Magadi**, a
soda lake in the Rift that attracts
flamingos and other lake birds
in the nearby swamps. It is a
place of soaring temperatures, a
source of soda and salts, and
there are hot springs beyond
the town at the edge of the
extraordinarily coloured ponds
and flats. You can walk on the
causeways, but beware of the
heat and wear a hat.

◆

THIKA
*off the main road to Mount
Kenya from Nairobi*
Thika, made famous by Elspeth
Huxley's novel *The Flame Trees*

of Thika, is an ordinary,
spreading industrial town. You
are more likely to be impressed
with the local crops of sisal and
pineapple than the famous trees
with their seasonal blaze of red
bloom. Local attractions include
**Ol-Doinyo Sabuk National
Park**, a 'Hill of Buffalos' but best
known for its birdlife, wide-
ranging views to Mount Kenya
from the top, and the falls on the
River Athi. The **Fourteen Falls**
are about 12 miles (20km) from
Thika with views of the
cataracts as you walk down the
path.

Accommodation
The two principal places to stay
in Naivasha are the independent
Safariland Club (tel: (0311)
20241) and the **Lake Naivasha
Hotel**, South Lake Road; book
through Block Hotels, Nairobi
(tel: 334807). Both are on the
lake with views and large
grounds loud with bird song.
There are good campsites and,
for bargain hunters, the **YMCA**,
a simple self-catering place not
far from the water.
Watch out for hippos wandering
up from the lake!
In Nanyuki, the **New Silverbeck
Hotel** (tel: Nanyuki 22710) offers
self-catering chalets.
There is a variety of places to
stay at Nyeri, including the
old-style **Thomson's Falls
Lodge** (tel: (0365) 22006) built
when the now defunct rail
line arrived, and situated close
to the town.
In Thika, the **Blue Posts Hotel**,
Muranga Road (tel: (0151) 22241)
is set in attractive gardens
overlooking two waterfalls. The
Safari Park is new.

LAKE VICTORIA AND THE WEST

Lake Victoria, the extreme western corner of Kenya, is Africa's largest freshwater lake, but is little known by visitors. This is due, in part, to the closeness of Uganda, which has had a well-publicised violent past, discouraging much tourism. But roads are fairly good, and the rail from Nairobi terminates here, and for the adventurous, this lakeside land offers much.

The area is the home of the Luo, originally herdsmen and fishermen, and Kenya's third largest tribal grouping.

There are marvellous game parks here, including the vast and very popular Masai-Mara. There are also the **Nandi Hills**: high, cool, tea-growing and attractive (much of Kenya's sugar and tea comes from this area); and the ancient primeval jungle to the north of Kisumu.

You could try taking a ferry to nearby shore towns and islands – these are run by Kenya Railways and have regular, cheap and prompt sailings daily (except Thursdays and Tuesdays for some destinations) to and from Kisumu. They are rarely crowded, and offer a safe and unusual way to see the country and the people.

◆
ELDORET
inland about 60 miles (96km) from Kisumu to Kitale
This large agricultural centre is

a junction of communications to Kitale and the Ugandan border. There is a healthy industrial sector and **Moi University**, one of Kenya's newer educational establishments, is based here.

HOMA BAY
south shore of Winam Gulf
A quiet and dull little place; but you can stay here and make a visit, using your own transport, to the **Lambwe Valley** and the fascinating newly-created Ruma Reserve. This is a place few tourists penetrate, home of the large roan antelope (attempts have been made to introduce this impressive beast to other parks) and the rare Rothschild's giraffe.

Follow Mbita Road for entry, left, to the reserve.

Admission charge per person plus car.

KAKAMEGA
about 20 miles (32km) up the road to Kitale from Kisumu
This small town is the jumping-off place for visits to the **Kakamega Forest**, a rare survival of a pocket of equatorial jungle, with many birds and unusual small mammals and reptiles (escorted walks possible: ask at the Forest Rest House). If you are willing to travel, you will find peace here (though the great blue turacos are hardly quiet birds!) and few people.

The town has a **library** and a **market**. In November the Agricultural Society of Kenya has a show for three days.

A giraffe stops for a snack

Leopards usually spend some of the day resting in tree branches

◆
KERICHO
about 50 miles (80km) southeast of Kisumu
This is the tea centre of the country, and a good place to come to if you want to escape the often clammy heat of the shore. The town is not big, but it is compact and neatly laid out with trees and shrubs, and its position on a plateau means it gets rain and fresh breezes. The **Tea Hotel** is a well-known attraction (see page 42). Expect dusty air if you manage to visit the tea packing factory, **KETEPA** (not easy); it is a pleasure to escape with a drive to the local fields, where you can see pickers at work.
About five miles (8km) away is the **Chagaik Dam** and the nearby **Arboretum**, a large grove of trees from all over Africa. Take a picnic and explore the area or just sit by the lake.
The **Kiptariet Valley** gives an idea of the country before tea-growing took over. East is the little known

mountain country of the **Mau Escarpment**.

KISII
about 30 miles (48km) south of Kendu Bay
A small yet fast-growing hill town, fertile and lively, with a large sports stadium and club. The town is Kenya's centre for soapstone carving. You can buy it here, or, better still, go to **Tabaka** (south on the road towards Tanzania), where the quarries and the carvers are located. If you buy, remember, soapstone is *heavy*!
You can go from Kisii to Tanzania on an international bus service, but check.

KISUMU
on the lake, terminus of rail and Nairobi road
A large and pleasant town, even though it has been suffering economic blight for more than a decade.
Historically important as the rail terminus from Nairobi, it is a port and Kenya's third largest city, but has little life, having suffered from trade breakdowns. There are connections again with Tanzania (it is possible to take a ferry from here now).
The town does have a big **market**, and the new **Kisumu Museum**, on the Nairobi road, east of town, is a must, with quite impressive stuffed animals, and a collection of ethnographic items featuring local tribes (open daily, small entrance fee).
Nearby is **Hippo Point**, for lake

hinterland that have no sea coast and depend on it for supplies. Its population is well in excess of half a million, many crowded on to the coral-rock island of less than six square miles (15 sq km) set in wetlands beside the Indian Ocean, and surrounded by gently rising land. To one side are the affluent suburbs of the north, linked to the mainland by a modern road bridge; to the northwest the industrial area and docks of Kilindini; to the west the airport, linked to Mombasa Island by the Kiperu Causeway; and to the east Mombasa harbour and, eventually, the open sea. The lands to the south are still relatively cut off from development, in the absence of a bridge, and depend on the lumbering Likoni Ferry service. (In fact Mombasa had no bridges at all until a century ago, and access was only by boat, or by fording the shallows.)

To discover Mombasa it is best to go on foot; the traffic and press of people makes it hard to see much from the windows of a vehicle. Walking is not that easy, either: the pavements are often broken and lodged with rubbish, especially off the main thoroughfares, where narrow streets are overhung with old houses.

Many shops are set up on the pavements, from car and bicycle repairs to stalls selling refreshments. Walking can be a slow business but by no means uninteresting, as you are pressed to buy or partake, or cheerfully greeted by

shopkeepers and artisans with calls of *Jambo*.

The atmosphere is much pleasanter than Nairobi, and not at all sinister, as can be the case in the capital.

A Walk Through Mombasa

From the main railway station on its parking lot, before the traffic oval of **Jubilee Square**, cross the tiny urban park and enter broad Haile Selassie Road, which will take you into the centre of Mombasa and the **Old Town**. A detour to the left and the **Mwembe Tayari Road** takes you to the principal bus departure points and **Makupa Street market**, where local food is prepared outside and the smells are very enticing. You could also stroll along **Biashara Street** (between Jomo Kenyatta Avenue and Abdel Nasser Road) where African merchandise is sold, including some very unusual and brightly designed fabrics. Haile Selassie Road takes you to the principal **Digo Road**, which slants across the city from north to south, joined at one point by the broad Kenyatta Avenue from the west.

The **Hindu Temples** give an exotic touch to Mombasa, with their brilliantly painted friezes and towers, and the Hindus seem pleased at any interest in their places of worship. Just off Mwembe Tayari Road is a large **Sikh Temple**, and there is a pastel-coloured **Jain Temple** on Langoni Road; while on Haile Selassie is the **Swaminaryan** temple of 1955.

It is more difficult to enter

An eye-catching shop in Ndia Kuu

mosques, and you may find them closed or not welcoming, particularly to women. You will need to be properly attired, and you may have to wash your feet as well as taking off your shoes.

Haile Selassie ends in Digo Road, with its odd, blue-globed **Triumphal Arches**. There are many roadside stands here, and tailors sit stitching on the pavements. Some of the older buildings are attractive, if grubby, examples of colonial styles; some are closed and desolate. Nevertheless, they offer fine photographic possibilites.

To the left are the streets of the **Old Town**, occupying the southeastern quarter of the island. This area is not too different from the rest of the city, but there are a few interesting balconied buildings once you get beyond the large and brassy banks, consulates and commercial buildings lining **Nkrumah Road**. There is also a large **market**, and the huge new **Bohra Mosque**

looms up to the left.

At the end of Nkrumah Road as you come to the edge of the island, you arrive at the **Ndia Kuu**, where there are many curio shops. This is the Fort Jesus area: from here return to the Old Town, or stroll to the end of **Dedan Kimathi Avenue**, where a little park makes a good place to pause and watch children play organised games beside a fountain and huge, creeper-draped trees.

Dedan Kimathi Avenue leads back to town and curls round the **Sports Ground**, a quiet spot with an affluent suburban character, despite the bad road.

Alternatively, you could follow the busier Nkrumah Road, heading past the **New Palm Tree Hotel** on the left and continuing past shops and offices until it arrives at the broad **Moi Avenue**.

Two of the social centres of Mombasa are nearby: the

Manor Hotel, on Nyerere Avenue, and the prominent and newly renovated Castle Hotel, with its white arches and terrace, is a popular and crowded meeting place. Prostitutes tend to frequent the area in the evenings.

Smaller hotels cluster nearby, with other local meeting places, such as the Kenya Coffee House, and the offices of the British Council are here. Head down the avenue, trying to ignore the numerous offers of assistance, from shoe-cleaning to taxis, and the occasional tout suggesting illegal exchange rates, or even offering to buy the clothes off your back.

New shops can be found in such developments as the Diamond Trust House, a long, white building to the left, in a sort of squashed classical style. To the right here is a small public garden. Uhuru Park, which is a bit desolate, and has almost been taken over by mediocre souvenir stands of every description. There is a central fountain, usually dry, shaped like Africa.

Turn right off Moi Avenue if you want to get away from this crowded thoroughfare. Here you will find local shops and restaurants; and you may be tempted to buy a picnic of grilled meats from backyard stalls along this road, especially in the early evening. Their delicious cooking smells compete with the malodorous chicken-and-crow-haunted rubbish piles. A short walk to the main cross street will bring you within sight of the railway station, over to your left.

WHAT TO SEE

◆◆◆
FORT JESUS ✓

Old Town

This 400-year-old fortress encapsulates, as nowhere else, the history of the intriguing island city. It is surprisingly well kept up and offers a cool place to walk in the shade of its walls, eight feet (2.4m) thick in places, and rising abruptly from a coral platform. From the water it gives an impression of sheer walls and impregnability, yet 'Jesus of Mombasa', founded by Mateus de Vasconcelos in 1593, was the focus of numerous actions and sieges, and was held by a number of groups during its history. Its final surrender was in 1875, when it was taken by British forces, wresting it from the Arab commandant serving the Sultan of Zanzibar.

The fort then became a prison, until restoration and renovation

Fort Jesus, a Portuguese relic

were commenced in 1958 with a grant from the Gulbenkian Foundation, based in Portugal. Two years later the fort was opened to the public as a national historic site and a museum.

You can easily spend half a day exploring the castle itself and wandering round the small yet well-varied **museum** within its walls.

The museum occupies the site of the soldiers' barracks, and among its exhibits are curios and objects retrieved from the wreck of a Portuguese ship, *Santo Antonio de Tanna*, which was trying to break a prolonged siege of the stronghold by Omani forces. This most famous and dreadful of all the actions seen by the fort lasted for two years and ended in 1698.

There is also a show of pottery recovered along the coast, some pieces over a thousand years old and woodwork which includes a fine carved Arab door from the town of Gazi on the south coast.

The fort also contains an **Omani Arab House**, carefully restored.

Open: every day 09.30–18.00hrs; admission charge.

LAW COURTS

Old Town

The new Law Courts building, with a grille and bougainvillea growing over the entrance, is strikingly designed (you can enter freely) and has a charming indoor tropical garden.

MAMA NGINA DRIVE

eastern shore of Mombasa Island

If you feel energetic and it's hot in town, take a long walk along the landscaped Mama Ngina Drive, which skirts the south sea-side of the island, and is marked with an entry arch declaiming '25 Great Years of Independence', set up in 1988. The drive brings you, after an interesting scenic stroll with views across to the reef, to a whole forest of the mysterious thick-trunked baobab trees near the departure point for the Likoni Ferry.

There are many legends attached to the baobab tree in Africa, and this curiously shaped, very slow growing tree does seem as if it were artificial, with its stocky trunk, spiky branches and scarecrow look. One story suggests that the baobab could once move about, and, annoyed with its peripatetic jaunts the creator of the world uprooted it and replanted the tree upside down . . . .

MBARAKI PILLAR

off Mbaraki Road, at Kilindini Cliffs

Another interesting site is this phallic pillar tomb, of which little is known; it was probably a memorial. Surrounded by baobab trees, its slightly leaning, round column of stone and plaster on a square base is hollow and has a row of arrow slits. It may mark, according to an inscription, the burial place of a leader of one of the original tribes of Mombasa. It is thought to be 18th-century.

The Jumbo Tusk Arch is a rivetting attraction for many visitors

◆
CATHOLIC MEMORIAL CATHEDRAL OF THE HOLY GHOST
Nkrumah Road

Here, in a stately position, is the principal Catholic church, with its barrel-vaulted roof. The site of the cathedral was purchased in 1891 by a priest who arrived in the city disguised in Arab dress. He built the first church, later replaced with the cathedral. Its prime status was secured with a promise that the church authorities would also build the local roads, which they proceeded to do, using the same coral quarry for materials. The Anglican **Mombasa Memorial Cathedral** is less prominent, although it has twin towers and a silver dome.

◆◆
SHREE CUTCH SATSANG TEMPLE
Haile Selassie Road

As exotic as a vanilla ice cream sundae, this Hindu temple is entered through a plaster and wood gateway, all beautifully painted in lurid colours.

Inside the temple is a wide and delightfully cool court, and upstairs is a large room with a coffered ceiling (you must remove your shoes before going upstairs).

It is worth taking the time to look at the brightly painted pictures, all in incredible detail and ranged around the walls, often gilded under their red and yellow arches. Friendly attendants are on hand to answer questions and provide information.

◆◆
THE TUSK ARCH
Moi Avenue

Ahead of you as you walk down busy Moi Avenue is Mombasa's most photographed sight: the two pairs of giant tusks that arch right over the avenue. These were erected in honour of Queen Elizabeth's Coronation

The popular Castle Hotel

in 1952, and are actually made of rivetted sheets of thin metal like an old-style aircraft fuselage.

On Moi Avenue, near the tin tusks, is the official **Mombasa Tourist Information** office in a low, single-storey corner building. The helpful staff will suggest hotels and guesthouses and provide information on excursions to the nearby game parks and reserves through local travel agents. The office is open Monday to Friday 08.00hrs–noon and 14.00–16.30hrs; Saturday 08.00hrs–noon).

◆

WOODCARVERS' VILLAGE

on the route to the airport
The sprawling Kamba carvers' area is an interesting place for a brief visit. Woodwork of mediocre quality is on display, but gives the impression of being cut from a hoary old pattern. It is better to look for more individual artists in the markets of Mombasa.

The carvers' village will, however, give you an idea of current prices and what you might expect to pay for a conventional souvenir; and there is certainly a lot to look at here.

Accommodation

The city has a number of small hotels, ranging from fair to budget prices. It also has two very good quality hotels.

The **Castle** (tel: 312558), in an imposing position on Moi Avenue, is known throughout Kenya, and has a terrace which is popular for snacks, coffee and meetings.

The **Manor** (tel: 314843) is also near Moi Avenue, at Nyerere Avenue, and has a number of cavernous public rooms and a terrace, but there is a friendly atmosphere here.

Being a port, and not a tourist city, Mombasa's central accommodation is limited, and many visitors stay outside town in the luxurious hotels along the south and north coasts. However, there are numerous small guesthouses in the city, useful for those on a budget or wanting to see Mombasa life at first-hand. For a medium price base try **The Outrigger** (tel: 220822), not central but quite cheap. The **Shelly Beach Hotel** (tel: 451001) is a budget hotel on the beach, about two miles (3km) from the ferry terminal at Likoni and set in gardens.

The tourist office on Moi Avenue can suggest possibilities for accommodation in all price brackets.

Restaurants

Far and away the best place in Mombasa (some say the best in Kenya!) is the expensive but wildly romantic **Tamarind Restaurant**, which is situated on the water in the suburb of Nyali – see pages 60 and 64 (reservations necessary; tel: Mombasa 471747). This is a 'must' for visitors, a tourist attraction in its own right. Food is spicy and Indian-based, but includes wonderful seafoods and shellfish, presented with great flair.

Mombasa's cuisine is certainly not bland: Asian influences see to that! The local fish, fruit and vegetables, such as plantain, beans, coconut and cassava, are much used and relished, and Indian spices add that special Swahili-coast taste. Although they can be quite expensive, fabulous grilled meat, prawns and warm-water lobster feasts are different and delicious here.

Mombasa is one place where hotel food is recommended: try the top floor restaurant and bar of the **Hotel Splendid**, for example.

Shopping

The Kamba wood carvers' market along the airport road will give you an idea of what's on offer, and you might also look carefully round the craft market on Moi Avenue. Shops on **Digo Road** have a vast array of clothing (mostly cheap and ordinary), but for fabrics that can be very attractive, and a bargain, try the bazaars along **Biashara Street**, off Kenyatta Avenue.

Fabric design is an art here, with wild and highly coloured patterns, supposedly fast-dyed. Take time to browse and bargain – you may be tempted.

At **Mackinnon Market**, besides fruit, vegetables and flowers, there are all kinds of spices on sale.

The location competes with the food at the Tamarind Restaurant

EXCURSIONS FROM MOMBASA

West of Mombasa, the interior extends from the flat shoreline to the hills, with **Mariakani** marking its edge. A large shallow bowl of land, it is the country of the Mijikenda

Craftsmanship and tradition combined in a tribal mask

people, a fairly loose group of tribes, speaking a Swahili-related tongue, with the Giriama and the Digo in the majority. This area is easy to get to from Mombasa, by car or by the frequently running *matatus*. It is much cultivated here, but still scenically very attractive. Long creeks and shallow lagoons finger in from the coast from Mombasa Island and Jumba, providing wide marshy areas, and the elegant coconut palms grow everywhere in this pleasingly hilly country. Towns such as **Kaloleni**, to the north, ordinary enough in themselves, have the attraction of sweeping scenery and wide-ranging views. In this country you can taste the *tembo*, or palm wine, and see the brew being collected from the fruiting stems of the palm, which are tapped for the sap. It is usually possible to buy a bottle of palm wine in bars if you wish to try it. The wine tastes better when it is cold, though it is often drunk tepid; in any case, you're not likely to become addicted: this is very much a local taste.

Mazeras is a pleasant little town at the edge of the Mombasa 'bowl', with an unusual Botanical Garden, and a local stop for the train. There is a large mission church here.

On the road north of Mazeras are **Rabai** and **Ribe**, two villages with mission histories. Rabai has a large **church** to mark its importance as the first mission of the area. It was founded in 1846 by a Pastor Krapf and is still used for worship.

THE NORTH COAST

Closer to the city of Mombasa than south coast hotels, because of the better connections (direct roads and bridges), the north shore resorts are easily approached on generally good roads.

Because of this ease of access the north has become more developed than the south and is now a pleasant, fairly well planned area, housing many of the city's better-off residents, especially in the suburb of Nyali (see page 60–61), which has many attractions in its own right.

A good road (the B8) runs from Mombasa to Malindi (see page 58), parallel to the coast; most of the attractions on the North Coast can be reached via this road.

♦♦♦
BAMBURI ✓

five miles (8km) north of Nyali and left off the main north road
This straggling settlement has a splendid attraction in the **Bamburi Nature Trail**. The trail is an attempt by the giant Bamburi Cement Company to re-use land devastated by quarrying for limestone, and it is a brilliant success. The area that was once almost lunar is now filled with foliage and a series of pools for fish-farming. It is a natural zoo, with animals in large, simply fenced areas, well wooded and as natural as possible. If you have no chance to go to a game park and see the beasts on the hoof, this is a

most acceptable alternative. Animals you should see are antelope (including the noble eland), giant tortoise, buffalo, hippo, crocodile, buck and zebra, as well as smaller creatures such as the

THE NORTH COAST

elegant serval cat.

Dozens of birds appear along the trail, which is an easy one to walk. There are snakes, too, and a fish farm with huge, many-coloured tilapia. Allow at least half a day, and if you go in the afternoon wait for feeding time at about 16.00hrs.

The trail was begun almost 20 years ago, and a totally natural look has now been achieved. Recently opened, adding an extension of the trail with imaginative re-use of the old quarries, is a huge new tract. This re-cycling is worth supporting. A very worthwhile project and a bargain too: the entrance fee is very reasonable. *Open*: every day 09.00–17.00hrs. Admission charge.

◆
BOMBULULU
near the entrance to the Nyali Toll Bridge

A centre for training disabled Kenyans to make jewellery and grow plants and fruit on the farm training area. The participants reside here for two years,

A hippo at Bamburi, a nature trail on land reclaimed from quarries

during which they learn new skills. There is a large shop selling the school produce, and you can view the weaving and jewellery-making and explore the gardens.

Open: every weekday from 08.00hrs; free.

GEDI
about half a mile (1km) down a track to the left from the modern village of Gedi; off the main B8 Mombasa-Malindi road

A very important early Swahili site. The jungle trees embrace and threaten to overwhelm the extensive ruins of Gedi, and, indeed, a riot of arboreal growth hid the settlement from foreign eyes for many decades before it was first discovered a century ago.

Detailed investigation did not come until 1948, but now it is a major attraction, even though a strange, sinister atmosphere seems to have attached itself to the walled ruins of a town that may have had up to 3,000 inhabitants at its zenith. Its population was wealthy, to judge from its remains (gems and beads from abroad, painted glass, ivory, and even aids to make-up have all been found). But it was mysteriously deserted in the 16th century, after an apparently prosperous growth, and nobody knows why this sophisticated settlement grew up or why it was placed here.

A guidebook about the site was written by the first excavator, Dr Kirkman, and this is useful to carry round with you along the arched paths and waist-high ruins.

There are 14 single-storey houses, walls, mosques (seven in all, allowing worship by both sexes) and tombs, as well as a large and complicated palace – all parts of the permanent stone core, although many of the residents must have occupied long-vanished mud huts to one side of the town. The houses had surprisingly good bathrooms, there are even bidets.

There is also a small museum on site, giving some idea of how the inhabitants lived and traded.

Open: all year round during daylight hours. Admission charge.

At the entrance to the Gedi ruins there is a **folk village** demonstrating local Giriama arts, such as drumming and dancing.

The **Arabuko Sokoke Forest** is to your left, approaching modern Gedi. The vast tract of jungle is impressive, and although slowly being decimated by seekers of hardwoods, there is still plenty of it left.

It is the haunt of many birds and small mammals, as well as the inevitable monkeys, and lots of butterflies and other insects. Take a detailed map if you venture in along the cool and inviting forest trails. It is not difficult to get lost in this thick, low-lying woodland (see also page 99).

◆◆
JUMBA LA MTWANA
half a mile (1km) north of Mtwapa Bridge (11 miles/18km from Mombasa); well signposted

Jumba ('The Large House of the Young Male Slave') is an ancient Swahili site of the 15th century, close to the beach and with several mosque ruins. It was disinterred in 1972, but little is known of the people who lived here, and much of the simple mud housing has vanished, leaving only the stone buildings.

Bamburi, a must for rock python fans

Wander along the rough road beyond the ticket office and explore the walls, cisterns and tombs on your own. Afterwards you could visit **Jumba Beach**, beyond the fat baobab trees, where curious high-rooted mangroves grow in the sand by the sea (site open all year; small admission charge).

Mtwapa Creek marks the official municipal boundary at the edge of Mombasa's 'country'. Before reaching the Creek you can find public beaches such as **Kenyatta Beach** (near Bamburi), off the road to the right, which are often quiet and relatively empty, especially during the week. You pass **Shantu Beach** to cross Mtwapa Creek – once crossed by a 'singing ferry', so-called because the ferrymen sang as they hauled on the cable. The Creek is now bridged.

KILIFI

36 miles (57km) north of Mombasa

Kilifi is a splendidly pretty place, with wooded shores pressing down to narrow beaches and sea water of an amazingly brilliant and clear blue. There are fine views down to the Creek and the lumbering ferries carrying traffic (free five-minute crossing, round the clock service) into Kilifi town from the docks below.

Kilifi depends for most of its trade on the cashew (there's a processing factory you could try visiting; the small, neat trees can be seen all over town) and coconuts, as well as sisal.

The local tribe is the Giriama, whose women used to go topless and sport grass dresses, although nowadays these are more likely to be of bright, patterned cloth swung stylishly round the exaggerated hips. The few Islamic ruins of **Mnarani**, signed left just before Kilifi and above the Creek, has been open to the public since 1977. There are mosques and a very tall pillar tomb, but the site is of considerable importance because of its complicated and decorative Arabic inscriptions. Its inhabitants were, it is believed, killed off in a confrontation, possibly between the rival towns, Mombasa and Malindi; but like so many of these ancient towns, very little is known of their inhabitants and what happened to them.

LAMU ✓

211 miles (340km) north of Mombasa; 136 miles (220km) north of Malindi

You need to be a bit of a masochist to face the road journey to Lamu and the end of the North Coast. For most of the distance from Malindi it is very rough going, and you will need a special vehicle, although there is a regular bus.

Best to ask about flights to the Manda airstrip, that serves the Lamu archipelago, with views of the coast and archipelago from the tiny aircraft. A short boat journey takes you to Lamu Island. You can fly from Mombasa, Malindi or Ukunda, on the south coast. By road you need to allow lots of time, and although the scenery is not too impressive, you may see wild animals.

When reached across its sea-channel, among a pattern of islands, the town is a step back to another time. It is advertised as the genuine 'old Arab trading town', but is much more than that. Although an old atmosphere persists this is basically a 19th-century town. Ancient Lamu's name is not recorded until 1402; but before that settlers on nearby Manda Island left Islamic and Chinese artefacts in the 9th century, and the area has very ancient historic sites. The Portuguese arrived in the early 16th century, but failed to achieve dominance. Lamu has always had a rich mixture of nationalities, and people passing through have had a tendency to stay on.

The area has a bizarre history and has always attracted the eccentric, both as residents and visitors. (There is even a pocket of transvestites.) The unconventional aspect of the town persisted right up to the 60's, when the African hippy trail wandered to an end here. The air of *laissez-faire* in Lamu and its surroundings is renowned. It is the perfect place to do nothing, cheaply and comfortably, and in an easy-going, agreeable style.

The Old Town is a fascinating place to explore on foot, with lots of palatial stone buildings and inner courtyards. Look for the carved doors of local mahogany and mangrove supports as you go – many

houses were built in the 17th and 18th centuries, when trade developed and the harbour was filled with loaded *dhows*.

The **waterfront**, with its verandas and mansions, is most attractive, yet quite recent. It was built on land filled in with rubbish in the last century, and makes a handsome introduction and screen to the much narrower alleys and passages of the Old Town beyond.

The relatively recent Arab **Sultan's Fort** was started by the Omanis in the early 19th century. It has had a number of uses, and is now cut off from its one-time-front-seat location on the old waterfront. It is now the island prison.

Guarded by an old British cannon, the town's **museum** contains two items that are worth the price of entry alone: ceremonial horns (*sivas*) – one brass, one ivory – which are symbols of kingship. These *sivas* may be the oldest musical instruments in East Africa. There is also a whole series of presentations of Swahili life and culture, as well as rooms devoted to other mainland tribes. There are many old photographs, one showing the town from the air – handy, in such a secretive place (open every day; closed lunchtimes; admission charge).

A **pillar tomb**, probably 14th-century, stands close to the Riyadha Mosque. There is another interesting tomb, much mutilated, in the town centre. The **Riyadha Mosque** itself is one of the most interesting, though almost the most recent, of Lamu's two-dozen mosques. Turquoise and green, with frilly decorations and filigree windows, it was built in the early part of the 20th century and is the town's largest centre of a very free and lively style of worship. The founder of the mosque, Habib Salih, also set up next to it an academy, a college for students of the Koran (usually always open – to suitably dressed men).

Around Lamu

Time is needed, but there are very good excursions available from Lamu.

Manda Island is a beautiful beach, and you can only reach it by *dhow. Dhow* cruises with a beach picnic included go from Lamu. You can also visit the ancient site of **Takwa**, supposedly the oldest of the entire coast.

Matandoni is the main centre on Lamu Island for the construction of the elegant *dhows*, although not much work is done on them now. It is a walk, or a donkey ride, from the town.

The small settlement of **Shela** on Lamu Island was once the town's main harbour. The most notable landmark is the Friday Mosque, with a rocket-shaped minaret (1829) and the Lamu beach is on the way.

If you have lots of time a visit to **Pate Island**, a truly deserted place with a particular charm and character all its own, is worth considering. It is a couple of hours by boat from Lamu and it makes a fascinating trip. You can also visit the famed **Nabahani Ruins**, founded by Arabs arriving here in the 13th

or 14th century. Visit **Pate Town**, a tightly laid-out settlement with locals dressed in their worldly wealth of gold and silver nose- and ear-rings.

You can really only walk to **Siyu** from Pate – but it is worth the effort along a rough track. There is a fort and a number of carved doors and further on through rough, scrubby terrain, the ancient site of **Shanga**. You will need a local guide.

MALINDI

74 miles (120km) north of Mombasa

The coast from Watamu (see page 62) up to Malindi is a Marine National Reserve, with two sections of this 80-square-mile (207 sq km) area making up the Watamu and Malindi Marine National Parks.

Malindi does have other attractions, too, although most of its tourists are there for the sun and the beach, and the town tends to be very crowded during the busy times of the European winter.

Malindi was the target of invading Portugese in the late 15th century, and although it went through a long quiescent period, it is now being invaded again. For a time it had the reputation of being a sex centre, but the advent of AIDS has diluted that. Now the invaders come for the watersports, which in July and August, when high winds drive in the sea, can include surfing.

The **Old Town** is not particularly interesting, and can be seen in a

Deserted sand dunes at Malindi

short time. There is a good **market**, and the **Swahili Quarter** merits attention; otherwise the real attractions are the sea and the reefs. This is a place to set out on fishing expeditions, and the town once played host to Ernest Hemingway when he stayed at the Marlin, one of the major hotels.

Fishing types come here for 'the big ones', and the deep sea fishing is reckoned to be as good as any of the Kenyan ocean ports. The best fishing times are September until April.

The ornate **Juma (Friday) Mosque** is the most notable of the dozen in town. Until a century ago it was also the site of a slave auction. Hassan's **pillar tomb** is 15th-century. **Malindi Marine National Park** should not be missed. Sail out over the Barracuda Channel to the amazing coral gardens of the **North Reef**, which has a vast selection of fish and reef-dwellers, as well as a variety of types of coral. Other good spots are the **Barracuda Reef**, and, deeper for the more adventurous diver or snorkeller, **Stork Passage**. If you prefer the quiet and ease of a glass-bottomed boat, you will still see an enormous amount of marine life as you glide over the clear water (open all year round; admission charge from embarkation at Casuarina Point. Best times: October to March at low tide).

Just outside the town, to the south, is the **Vasco da Gama Pillar and Monument**. The simple, short pillar's location on an exposed clifftop makes it well worth a visit. Malindi also has a modern (1960) cement monument to the explorer, who arrived in 1498: a simple sail of the period with a mast. He passed through Malindi on his way to India, and there is a **Vasco da Gama Church**, notable mainly for its age: it was built in 1541, and forms part of a 16th-century chapel.

Around Malindi

Some distance from the town, but a popular outing, **Hell's Kitchen** is a geological oddity: a deeply eroded zone of pink, brown and orange rock. You can walk through it, along precipitous paths, to see the fantastic formations close up. The raw earth colours are strong and encompass cliffs and pinnacles.

Inland from Malindi is the village of **Mambrui**, with its ornate domed mosque, bright ice-cream green and white. This is another popular day-trip from the resort, being only about eight miles (14km) away. There is a pillar tomb: it's worth a look for its inset late period Ming porcelain bowls.

For a long outing, you could go from Malindi to visit one of Kenya's most remote and awe-inspiring parks. Take the road marked for Kakaoneni and Tsavo to reach **Tsavo East**, which has several gates, the most popular being along the Mombasa–Nairobi road. Most people enter the park from Voi or Tsavo on the western side. A huge and forbiddingly dry game park, **Tsavo East** is also one of the least-visited, and a large northern part is completely closed to the public.

Tsavo, Kenya's largest wildlife wilderness

It seems almost depressingly empty, now that poachers have decimated elephant and rhino herds, and yet it has a magical air of real Africa. You are apt to be all on your own as you drive through on the Malindi-Mombasa road track (beyond the main rail and road lies the more popular Tsavo West) and there are only a couple of places to stay – try the well-sited **Aruba Lodge**, close to the Voi River.

Arriving at Tsavo East from Malindi means a long, often rough and rather dull drive to the increasingly used **Sala Gate**, beside the Galana River. Here there are crocodiles and a game ranch, offering a chance to see an experimental conservation project, involving both cattle and wild game.

Alternatively, arriving from Voi you enter by the Voi Gate. The other entrances to Tsavo East are the Buchana Gate (south of Voi on the Nairobi/Mombasa Road) and the Manyani Gate, nine miles (15km) south of Tsavo Station on the Nairobi/Mombasa road.

ARABUKO SOKOKE FOREST
18 miles (30km) north of Mombasa
A stretch of ancient forest land off the Malindi Road. Home to birds and many small mammals, including rare bats.

NYALI
across the New Nyali Toll Bridge from Mombasa
This is essentially a large, smart suburb of Mombasa, although

separated by water. Laid out with wide streets, lawns and gardens. Nyali has a seafront looking over Dhow Harbour to the skyline of Mombasa. It has resort hotels along its beach and a good number of shops and attractions. Even if you are not staying at expensive hotels, hoteliers usually don't mind if you use their beaches and bars. Hotel food tends to be international in style, so if you are unsure of local food you can eat well at the hotels' buffet tables. The Nyali hotels operate private bus services into town; the journey takes less than 15 minutes.

Dhow Trip ✓

A *dhow* trip operates from the Tamarind Quay on Nyali's waterfront. This authentic Arab trading *dhow*, or *jahazi*, provides a marvellous journey onto the waters of the harbour and around the island. One of the largest *dhows* in Kenya, it was built in 1977 in Lamu, using traditional woodworking methods, and manned by local sailors from that area; until 1986 it was a working cargo *dhow*. It can be hired for periods, or you can take a lunch cruise from the Tamarind; the meal is cooked on a charcoal grill on board from local recipes. You can watch the sailors sail the ship, first under power and then using the great triangular sail which is caught up in authentic manner to its spars, using a kind of dried raffia as a series of ties. It's quite a sight when these break, all at once, and the sail bellies out (morning cruise at 10.30hrs,

returning 14.45hrs, lunch included in fee; dinner cruise departs 18.30hrs, returns 22.30hrs, dinner and dancing to live band included in fee. Lunch only, pick-up 12.30hrs; group bookings for up to 100 people). Information is available from **Tamarind Dhow**, PO Box 99456, Mombasa; tel: 220990.

Frere Town is the next suburb to Nyali. Those interested in history will welcome the chance to visit the **Emmanuel Church**, a pink-washed building where the Church Missionary Society had its headquarters until 1930. Freretown was one of the first sanctuaries for freed slaves, and the church bell frequently sounded to warn of Arab slave-trading *dhows* in the vicinity. One of the most famous of the emancipated slaves was Matthew Wellington, who accompanied Dr Livingstone on his extensive peregrinations. Eventually, when the explorer died, he conveyed the body back for burial on the coast. His portrait is in the vestry.

Mamba Village is well marked in central Nyali, and advertised all over the place. *Mambas* are crocodiles, and this is basically another view of a skin-farm with the original suppliers, in a range of ages, on view in a number of rock pools. Lots of souvenirs are on sale (check if you can import them home; animal products are often illegal) and if you are really intrigued you can try a crocodile meat burger in the café on site. Camel rides are also offered in the village (open every day, admission charge; tel: 472709).

THE NORTH COAST

◆
VIPINGO
15 miles (24km) north of Mombasa

The Mombasa–Malindi road passes through this small town, where sisal plants stretch away in long rows. There are over 20,000 acres (8,000 hectares) of the spiky plants – although production of this once important crop is declining. As you leave the ordered rows and long, low houses where the leaves are dried, you enter rougher hill country.

Just beyond the half-way point between Vipingo and Kilifi there is a turn to the right and it is three miles (5km) to the village of **Takaungu**, by the sea on its own creek, which is set between cliffs and is startlingly beautiful. This is well worth a detour and a picnic if you have time. A little further on a road runs south to the Mijikenda country and the town of Kaloleni.

◆◆◆
WATAMU
twelve miles (20km) south of Malindi

After skirting a series of lagoons and inlets known as **Mida Creek**, on the B8, you reach the turnoff at Gedi. Here there are mangrove swamps fringing the sea and, during the March–May period in particular, there are many wading and water birds to be seen (you will need to leave the road, however, to see the creeks properly). The best way is to take time and rent a boat to explore the snaking inlets and the

A plover on the coast at Malindi

particularly rich natural life of the lagoons.

Watamu is the shore-town along the Gedi road, a modern resort with hotels and craggy coral-rock headlands, lagoons and a beach of palest pink sand known as Turtle Bay.

It is a resort village which has grown up from a simple settlement, and now the resort area boasts several hotels, with visitors eager to visit the renowned **Watamu Marine National Park**. Stretching from the Blue Lagoon to Mida Creek, this area of ocean has been a marine park since 1968. The best time to visit the coral gardens is the period between October and March, although you can see them at any time. It is a parade of colour – fantastic corals and luminous fish in water that is so clear it hardly seems real, as the glass-bottomed boat steals over the surface. You can also dive down and join the fishy ranks, of course (open all year; admission charge).

Just near the entrance to the Mida Creek lagoons is an underwater set of caverns called the **Tewa Caves**. Here, in the 'Big Three Caves', lurk several enormous grouper (the *tewa*), reaching up to six feet (1.8m) and weighing over 500 pounds (226kg). These giant fish hang motionless in the water, about 10 feet (3m) down, depending on tides.

You can see the Tewa caves as part of the Mida Creek boat trip.

Accommodation

The charming **Serena Beach Hotel** at Shanzu, 12½ miles (20km) north of Mombasa (tel: 485721) has accommodation in handsome little buildings grouped in gardens, and with its own craft-makers' centre. Very much a package-holiday place, as are almost all of Kenya's coastal hotels, it does have real character. There is a good, if rather narrow beach here.

Jumba

A short distance from Jumba is the settlement of **Kikambala**, with its youth hostel. It is on a very fine, broad beach, backed with trees. A good place to picnic, but stop for supplies at one of the dukas on the main road.

The **Whispering Palms** (tel: Kikambala 32620) is set in woods near the beach. Beaches here are often deserted, the disadvantage being that they usually lie a little way off from the main road, so you may have to hike down rough tracks to get to the sea. Once there, however, you are not likely to be disappointed.

Kilifi

The **Seahorse Hotel** (tel: (01252) 9064) is a draw for would-be sailors and yachtsmen.

Lamu

The **Peponi Hotel** (tel: (0121)

Bordering land and sea, mangrove swamp forests are renowned for their salt-impregnated timber

3029) is a quality place to stay outside the town: the island's top spot. Try also the **Petley's Inn** (tel: (0121) 48107), which has the island's only bar and is patronised by package tours. Also **Yumbe House Lodge** (tel: (0121) 3101). Otherwise accommodation is all self-catering.

Malindi
Driftwood Beach Club (tel: (0123) 20155) or the **Coconut Village** (tel: (0123) 20928).
Others: **Blue Bay Village** (tel: (0122) 32626), Eden Roc.

Nyali
The **Mombasa Beach Hotel** (tel: 471861) is recommended. Closer to town, the luxurious yet attractively old-style **Nyali Beach Hotel** has an air of grandeur and a very helpful staff. Book through Block Hotels, Nairobi (tel: 335807); **Watamu Turtle Bay** (tel: (0122) 32662).

Restaurants
Lamu
Try **Ghai's**, or the well-recommended **Equator** restaurant. Both are moderately dear, and specialise in seafood.

Nyali
Recommended is the beautifully placed **Tamarind Restaurant** (tel: 471747), with sea views and terraces.
Fish and shellfish are a speciality, and local methods of cooking are stressed, along with potent drinks such as the vodka and wild honey-based cocktail known as *hawa*.
Below you is a dock and, here, a great wooden *dhow*, the *Nawàlikher*, is often at anchor, adding another romantic touch to the occasion.

Shopping
In Lamu, look for intricate, Arab-style bone-and-ivory-inlaid chests; models of *dhows* (these unique vessels are still constructed here) and woodcarvings, as well as some novel local silverware designs.

Relaxing before a dip in the pool at the gleaming Mombasa Beach Hotel, Nyali

THE SOUTH COAST

Beyond Mombasa the south coast ambles down towards the Tanzania border, and a beautiful stretch of shoreline it is. Leaving Mombasa, you will need to take the ferry at **Likoni** from the island, to arrive at the main road south (the A14).

After crossing with loads of cars, *matatus* and people selling eggs and produce, you ascend a rough slope, and the road indicating Lunga Lunga (eventually) and the beach are before you. The road surface is good and driving easy, but watch out for sleeping policemen on some parts. You pass through several settlements, some rapidly becoming modernised with supermarkets and new houses, but many still simple and with a local air. Construction here consists of mud infill of wooden frames which look like cages; the huts are then thatched. The tribe here is the Digo, soft-spoken and neat-featured, part of the Mijikenda peoples.

There is a settlement at **Likoni**, but it is a rather run-down place, with a messy beach; basically a city suburb. From here the buses ply south. **Ngombeni** is a straggling village settlement, useful for buying supplies and services. It marks the right turn for Kwale. **Kwale** itself is about 11 miles (18km) along the road and is a large and prosperous village with an enormous green and meeting-shed in the middle.

If you are planning to camp at the Shimba Hills National Park (see page 68) you can obtain supplies here, and it is possible to stay very simply. The park is a short distance beyond the village, along a rough track.

The road south runs inland, but the strip of beach is never far away. The coastal plain is flat and very lush, with thick foliage and many baobab trees. Small turnings to the left take you to the sea in a matter of moments – the one marked for **Tiwi Beach**, just before Tiwi itself, will take you to the best resort closest to Mombasa. The beach is very good, with lots of graceful palm trees, and the sands run almost continuously from here, except for river estuaries, all the way south to Msambweni.

Just across the Tini River is the fascinating 15th-century **Kongo Mosque**, reached along a very rough track. This is one of the old relics of Islam that dot the shoreline of Mombasa, and Kongo is in surprisingly good condition under its barrel roof. Being stone-built, it has survived while other buildings of the era, built of less durable materials, have vanished. It is also known as the Diani Persian Mosque, and marks the northern edge of the resort strip known as Diani Beach (see below).

DIANI BEACH
east of the main A14 Mombasa–Lunga Lunga road
The main south coast road runs down to Ukunda, a straggling settlement with shops and

hotels, and excellent fresh fruit and vegetable stands useful for self-caterers.

Along the main road are signs to the left for Diani Beach. This is the strip that the brochures depict, glowingly blue and gold, with atmospheric palm trees along the beach and *dhows* dotted about on the clear Indian Ocean.

You turn left off the main road and arrive at a T-junction with a confusing clutter of signs, indicating a vast range of places to stay, from the cheap to the luxurious.

The beach, long and wide with shallow approaches, is what attracts most people to Diani – and it is a marvellous one, with fine sand and a clean sea lapping the edge. Offshore there is a reef, which can be walked to at low tide; otherwise there is no lack of small boats to take you there, some glass-bottomed to give a view of the fish.

Take a pair of rubber sandals when paddling, so that you don't cut your feet; and remember, too, that you can look for shells but not take – a recent law forbids the export of rare molluscs, so ignore the beach-boys trying to sell you a stunning sample. It may well be taken away at the airport if you succumb (an example of Kenya's concern about its fauna and flora, evident in many laws to protect a heritage that is vital).

On the beaches you can see Masai people trying to sell their spears and shields made for the tourist market. These men, noticeable for their tall, gaunt figures, sometimes have their hair done in classic Masai red-dyed and sculpted styles. Hotels offer Masai dancing on certain nights of the week.

You can hire reef equipment and go scuba diving at Diani, or try windsurfing or water skiing. (Lessons are offered, but these can be quite expensive, so shop around.) If the pleasures of the beach pall, you can hire a bicycle or a mini-moke for exploring inland.

Around Diani Beach

Just across the well-metalled road from the hotel strip the **Jadini Forest** takes over, and here, along tracks leading away from the sea, you will find all sorts of local creatures, from monkeys and the most beautiful butterflies to birds. (Do not, however, attempt to feed the monkeys you see wandering about the hotel gardens – they are dangerous and they bite.)

You will also see sleepy little local boys herding goats. This is the relic of the sea-marge woodland, and there is not a lot of it left. There are large hardwood trees, baobabs, and many flowering shrubs, and the woods echo with birdsong. At night, the glowing eyes you may see reflected in a flashlight are likely to be those of a bushbaby, although leopards are supposed to be fairly widespread in the hills beyond the coastal strip.

It is a pity that more is not being done to preserve this dwindling woodland, but tourism has brought much money to the area and hotels are expanding. A lot of their staff live off the tracks in the Jadini Forest.

South of Diani Beach there is quieter country. Turn left from the main Mombasa–Lunga Lunga road (the Diani Beach road only serves the hotels) for **Kimondo**, and its beach; and beyond this settlement the coast comes to an idyllic point in **Chale Island**, where you can be taken on special excursions for diving and a typical barbecue meal under the sun. It is a tiny place and, so far (apart from tourist boats), unspoiled. (All local tourist hotels offer packaged price visits.)

Returning to the main road, you next come to **Gazi**, just off the road, and so on to **Msambweni**, on a loop road down to its beach, which is backed with cliffs and not much discovered as yet.

South of here, and again off the end of a peninsula, is **Funzi Island**, much bigger than Chale, and which can be approached on foot from the coast path when the tide is low. There is a village here and reefs, as well as beaches and thick woods, so it could make a rough and ready place to stay if you fancy getting away from it all with the simple life of a desert island.

Return to the highway, passing more woodland until the lower levels break to reveal fields of sugar cane, as you pass the ancient settlement of **Shirazi**, once inhabited by the conquerors of the coast, who ruled from here. This is a place to see local life: a tiny settlement of scattered huts off the road, with Islamic connections still obvious in the ragged ruins of a mosque and fortifications vanishing into the undergrowth.

Shimoni comes next, marked to the left on the highway. Take the road down this wide peninsula to the small village at its southern end. Popular with fishermen, it also has a series of caves, from which the place derives its name. They are extensive and may once have been used for assembling and keeping slaves, before the Arab traders shipped the poor victims, plundered from inland villages, west.

Immediately off Shimoni is the long sliver of **Wasini Island**, easily reached from the dock by boat. It is small and beach-girt, and marvellous for walks, with lots of shells to see. There are pleasing small places to eat in the village, which also has a high-and-dry coral garden.

◆◆◆
THE KISITE-MPUNGUTI MARINE NATIONAL PARK ✓

a boat ride from Wasini Island (left off the Mombasa–Lunga Lunga road)

For the real, living, undersea corals, this is one of Kenya's marvels, and not to be missed. This long rectangle of clear water, which is a paradise for divers, is a unique spectacle. Several package trips are offered by hotels and

THE SOUTH COAST

A cinnamon-chested bee-eater

agencies from Wasini and further afield, often with an accompanying lunch of seafood as a grand picnic built into the price. It is not easy to find a place to stay here, but it is idyllic, and worth a visit, especially for the snorkellers who want to experience a real treat.

◆◆◆
SHIMBA HILLS NATIONAL RESERVE
about 10 miles (16km) inland from Kwale

A great attraction of the South Coast, and one that, oddly enough, is usually overlooked, is the magnificent Shimba Hills Reserve. The lodge is about eight years old and has been constructed like a tree-house, by two Nairobi architects. It is all beautifully rustic, yet comfortable, and is run with great style and efficiency by the resident warden, who will be happy if you are genuinely interested and intrigued with this lovely place.

The animals dispersed during the building operations, and maybe this is why some Kenyans will tell you that there is not much here – don't believe them, for there is a lot to see. The hotel-lodge surrounds a large pool, which is a dammed stream and is filled with waterlilies and water-birds. More importantly, the vegetation is thick and comes right down to the water, so that there is lots of cover for shyer animals.

The reserve is lush and rarely dry, so the water is not the big attraction here – but food is put out to attract the creatures. There is a long tree walk (you can take a drink and watch the forest floor below, as well as the insect life crashing into the lights) and another walk is planned. You eat well, if simply, at the lodge, with the view set out before you.

The drives take in the small yet very varied National Reserve. The park has some marvellous bird life, from hornbills to bee-eaters, with quite a lot of ground birds. Another great appeal is the sweep of far-ranging views.

You can see the interior as far as Kilimanjaro on a clear day, and, in the opposite direction, spectacular vistas of the sea and beach to the east, all the way down to Chale Island.

With the blessing of clear weather, a drive in Shimba in the early morning, or just before sunset, can be unforgettable, whether you go for the excitement of the animal and bird life, or just for the peace and quiet of the lodge.

To arrive here, take the road to Kwale, just south of Mombasa (well marked metalled road to the right), and within moments you are climbing up away from the heat and humidity of the coastal strip. You can visit Shimba by car or on a safari package. Although you can spend a day, or even half a day, a night at the lodge is recommended. Your visit includes overnight accommodation, dinner, bed and breakfast and game drives. If you have no transport to the park, then a bus going to Kinango from Kwale goes through the park.

Beyond this settlement there is open country and few roads all the way to Bura in the Taita Hills and Tsavo West. This used to be an elephant corridor, and the Shimba warden has an interesting tale about migrations still continuing.

Open: from 06.00hrs to sunset.

◆◆
VANGA
beyond Lunga Lunga
South of the Kisite-Mpunguti Marine Park, the south coast road continues to Lunga Lunga, which is really only a border post with Tanzania.

Beyond, and towards the sea, in a setting of mangroves and gleaming, marshy flats is Vanga, which is untouched by visitors, even though there are simple places to stay along the main street. This fishing village is ringed with small market gardening establishments and *shambas* set in lush countryside.

You can ask about exploring the gloomy mangrove swamps in a canoe, or search out the little beaches.

This is the most southerly point of the whole country, and Vanga has an air of being lost and out of the way – which can be of great appeal if you are looking for a curiously romantic spot, where there really is nothing else to do at all but sit and relax in the sun or explore.

Accommodation
Diani Beach
Taking its name from the local woodland, the **Jadini Beach Hotel** (tel: (01261) 3200) is typical of the 'luxury strip' and is all you would expect of a grand resort hotel, with very good service, extensive gardens and plenty of things for guests to do.

Other nearby hotels at the expensive end: the new **Kazkazi Beach** (tel: (0127) 3170), **Safari Beach** (tel: (01261) 2366), the **Two Fishes** (tel: (01261) 2101) and **Leopard Beach** with an Italian-style grill (tel: (0127) 2721).

Shimba Hills
The **Shimba Hills Lodge** can be booked through Block Hotels, Nairobi (tel: 335807).

Restaurants
Many of the hotels in Diani Beach are tied in to package holidays and, with the tourists staying half-board, there is not much incentive to go out and eat. However, good restaurants can be found along the 'strip'. Unlike the north shore, this area is quite a distance from Mombasa, so it is a fairly long journey into town to eat. You can often eat at other hotels on a holiday plan with your own, but locally renowned, although not cheap, is a strange place called **Ali Barbour's**, where there is a large menu and wine selection, and you will eat in a cave – with coral and a gaping hole in the roof, so that you can see the stars at the same time. For Indian tandoori fare try **Maharani** (tel: (0127) 2439).

Shopping
All the Diani Beach hotels will offer half-day shopping trips into town, as well as excursions to the islands using *dhows*, Shimba Hills visits, and even an expensive covered-wagon overnight trip.
There is also a regular hourly bus service from Mombasa; check with your hotel's information desk, or use taxi services.

The seaside Jadini Beach Hotel

Man's birthplace – the Rift Valley

THE RIFT VALLEY ✓

The Rift Valley is a vast fault in the continental make-up, which, in pre-history, was a large inland body of water. This is now a string of lakes. The area is like a fat finger pointing towards the Ugandan border, between the Nairobi area and Western Kenya.

◆◆
LAKE BARINGO
north on a good road, 75 miles (120km) from Nakuru
This large lake is fresh water and has a special character, making a sharply verdant contrast to the dry and eroded lands nearby. The lake itself is heavily loaded with local red topsoil and, as a result, the water reflects soft colours of lavender, pink and purple at different times of the day. With its low thorn trees along a wide flat shore, it makes a beautiful, often changing picture. There is a vast variety of birds, some quite rare, such as the Verreaux's eagle; but here even the commonest birds seem to attract attention.

There is a camp on the island of Ol Kokwa, and you can be taken there by motor boat.
Open: all the time; free.
Nearby is the newly-opened Kamncroc Reserve (with crocodile and elephants).

◆◆
LAKE BOGORIA
about 40 miles (64km) to the north from Nakuru
This salt water lake seems inhospitable at first, set amid grim hills (the Siracho range forms cliffs on the eastern edge). The bubbling of hot springs, in rocks and rough terrain, provide a harsh and often terrifying hot landscape, yet it is a fascinating place. Here you will also see flamingos.

Open: every day, dawn to dusk.
Admission charge.

◆
LAKE MAGADI
lower Rift Valley, southeast of Nairobi
A soda lake in the Rift that attracts flamingos and other lake birds in the nearby swamps. You can actually walk across the expanse of shallow flats, where the salt and soda are mounded into long ridges. A place of

soaring temperatures, with hot springs beyond the town.

◆◆◆
LAKE NAKURU NATIONAL PARK
five miles (8km) south of Nakuru (see below)
The enormous population of lesser and greater flamingos in this large water reserve may be as many as two million, but numbers are less predictable now, due to changes in the

Dawn at Lake Nakuru; curtain up on the greatest bird show on earth

migrants. The enlarging of the park has promoted the mammals too, bringing new arrivals. The most interesting 'immigrants' are the rhinoceros, the black species, brought to a safe environment and protected (as is the whole park, courtesy of the World Wide Fund for Nature) by a perimeter fence – a necessity in this era of unbridled poaching (also see entry on page 88).
Open: every day, dawn to dusk. Admission charge.

◆
NAKURU
midway between Nairobi and Kisumu
This is Kenya's fourth largest town, and the only big settlement in the Valley. It was also born as a railway baby, around 1900, and now serves as an agricultural centre for local farmers, mainly growers of pyrethrum for insecticides, who come in to buy necessities from the shops along its dusty, colonnaded streets. You can use it as a base for Rift exploration; there is not much to see, nor are there any leading hotels in town, but you can find cheap accommodation here (see page 74).
Behind the town of Nakuru rises a vast extinct volcano, with a caldera at its crest. This is the **Menengai Crater**, and you can climb up to it from the town. You will need to make it a day's visit if you walk, and be sure to take water and a picnic.

water composition, affecting algae growth. (This was amended in 1974 when the park was enlarged to prevent too much agricultural invasion.) The vast flocks of flamingos still make a heart-stopping sight when they take wing against the blue. (Their pink feathers are due to the colour of a small shrimp consumed as part of their algae diet.)
The park is a temporary home for many European bird

THE RIFT VALLEY

Also close to the town is **Hyrax Hill**, off to the right of the main Nairobi road. Possibly 3,000 years old, this ancient settlement site was excavated in the 1930s by Mary Leakey. Buy a guidebook at the Museum and walk the site. The ancient board games of *bau*, cut into the rock, are fascinating (open every day, small admission charge).

South of Nakuru is **Gilgil**, with its Commonwealth War cemetery. The graves are mostly from the African Campaign and the struggle for Independence. Between Gilgil and Nakuru lies Lake **Elementeita**, a wide and gleaming soda lake, where some flamingos may be seen. There are also prehistoric sites dotted around the shores.

Other sights in the Rift include the steep **Kerio River Valley**, and the dramatic **Elgeyo Escarpment** to the north. Further south, the **Mau Escarpment** forms a similar wall to the west beyond Nakuru. If you can get up to the top (the road is a challenge to any vehicle) you will be rewarded with an amazing vista stretching as far as Mount Kenya. Better to arrive at the top from Eldoret or Kitale to the west. Beyond are the **Charangani Hills** (approached off the Kitale–Lodwar road). Not surprisingly, they are not much visited and have a wild and untouched air. These lonely hills have empty moorland at their summits, yet they are a wonderful place to hike. Water from the hills is guided through ancient ducts down the escarpment. The *shambas* are, as a result, green and verdant places, packed against the base of the hills.

Accommodation

Lake Baringo Club (Block) and **Highland Camp** (Lonrho) are new, as is the 4-star **Lake Bagoria Hotel** (tel: 40896). For Kamnaroc, the **Kabarnet Hotel** (ATNH).

Sarova Hotels maintain the **Sarova Lion Hill** at Nakuru (tel: central reservations: 333233). Camping within the park is at designated spots.

The black rhino, now a rare sight

THE NORTH AND EAST

This is a part of Kenya most
visitors never see, yet it has its
share of attractions, even though
the traveller needs to be
intrepid to enter this strange
desert land. A glance at the map
will indicate that almost all of
Kenya's population and
development is along the
southwestern third of the
country. North and east of Mount
Kenya there extends a vast tract
of near-empty land, with hardly
any communications. As you
might expect, most of this area
is either desert or arid and
infertile, getting progressively
drier and sterner towards the
borders of Ethiopia and Somalia.
It is tough country, and only for
those who are determined to
see real back-country. Be
warned: the going is hard and
the travelling long and arduous,
often on almost non-existent
roads.

The North

You can find tours to take you
here, although you must allow
lots of time; usually a minimum
of a week. In addition, you will
need to be prepared and to
check carefully on what you
may find necessary in a part of
the country ill-supplied with
provisions. The watchword for
visits to this part of Kenya, right
up to the desolate Northern
Frontier district, as it was once
known, is preparation; you need
some knowledge of what you
are in for.

Camping safaris, complete with
cook, can take you up to
the eastern shore along very
rough roads; or you can elect to

*An African skimmer in quiet
reflection*

go on your own, but this
demands considerable self-
reliance and awareness of the
difficulties.

You should consider the fact
that your transport will often be
in four-wheel drive vehicles
over very bumpy terrain. Take
skin creams or emollients
against the inevitable chaffing
of backs and legs during jolting
journeys, and packets of
moistened tissues are
extremely useful, for many
places will have limited water
supplies, and the journey may
be hot and uncomfortable for
long periods.

If you intend travelling with
your own transport it is wise to
have a knowledge of possible
engine problems and you
should carry plenty of water, as
well as extra fuel.

Despite this necessary advice,
for many the north is one of the
most challenging and
memorable parts of the country.
The local people are the
Turkana, and they are an
individualistic and often
aggressive tribe. You will see
Samburu people too, in their
wrap-around blankets and
extraordinary metal and bead
bracelets and necklaces, some

of the men wearing red mud on faces and hair, like the Masai, a tribe they are related to. They live on the eastern shore, a cattle and camel herding people. You may also like to visit the El Molo – they live around the south end of the lake, a fish-eating, bow-legged people, and this smallest of tribes has its centre just outside **Loyangalani**, where they are quite welcoming to visitors.

◆◆◆
LAKE TURKANA
on the border with Ethiopia
Paramount attraction and focus of northern safaris, the long finger of Lake Turkana is a very unusual body of water, host to a variety of wildlife from hippos to huge Nile perch. These include the Turkana tiger-fish, famous to fishermen as great fighters, and many crocodiles, of the Nile variety. It is a station for bird migration, too, with flocks flying north before the heavy rains of May. Other birds are exotics such as flamingos, cormorants, cranes, pelicans, ibis and other waders.

Lake Turkana is in a pristine spot. It wasn't found until 1888, and its Austrian discoverers named it after the heir to the throne, Rudolf, a name it bore until 1975. Its shoreline is almost entirely within Kenya, but the northernmost shore forms part of the border with Ethiopia. The lake is something of a curiosity: nobody knows what caused it to be there, since it is now cut off from the Nile it once fed, and why, despite its

160-mile (257km) length and the fact that no rivers run from it, it is decreasing dramatically, with evaporation taking up to nine feet (3m) of its water every year. Originally huge, the lake is now a shadow of what it once was – a vast glittering desert sea.

You cannot drive round the lake, so you approach either from the west (from **Kitale**, a small agricultural town and focus for departures to the north along a new road to **Lodwar**, a boom-town and capital for the Turkana people); or from the eastern way through **Maralal**, frontier hill town and home of the Samburu, and on to **Loyangalani**, a tiny, isolated lake town on the southern shore.

It is also approachable from Marsabit to **Allia Bay**, on the edge of the Sibiloi National Park. In general the Marsabit route is not recommended except for the real adventurer.

If you haven't time, or can't face the long land haul, and you have the money, then you can fly from Nairobi's small Wilson airport, and the Air Safari trip does give magnificent views over this wild and unvisited country.

◆◆
SIBILOI NATIONAL PARK
eastern shore of Lake Turkana at Allia Bay
Largest of several national parks in the area, this area is hard to get to, edging the Chalbi desert and stretching up almost to the Ethiopian border. It is famous for its fossils, some of which can be seen in the

Abyssinian roller: a resident of northern Kenya

museum. In this bare, rocky and wind-scoured place, there are a lot of animals: you should see the shy gerenuk, which looks like a long-necked impala.

◆◆
SOUTH AND CENTRAL ISLAND NATIONAL PARK
southern and western shores of Lake Turkana

These two island parks are set in the dramatic Lake Turkana. South Island National Park, with brilliant green crater lakes indicating its volcanic origin, attracts colonies of nesting shore birds. Bigger than Central Island, it is approached from the small settlement of Loyangalani, and is not easy to get to.
Central Island is a major breeding ground for crocodiles and at hatching time (usually April) you can view the little crocs breaking out of their leathery shells, and making for the water with instant determination in their beady eyes.
Central Island is approached by boat from Kolokol or its nearby fishing lodge. There is a small admission charge.

The East
If the north seems inhospitable, then the east, a truly gigantic tract of land from the Nairobi-Isiolo-Marsabit-Moyale road towards the Somalian border, is near-desolation. Unrelieved wastes and deserts are punctuated with small and dusty townships, making a few dots on the otherwise bare map.
Local people are herders, moving cattle across dry plains under the wide skies of the desert. This country is for the traveller who wants to go where almost no-one else does.
You can travel for many miles to reach the border towns of **Mandera** (for Somalia) and **Moyale** (for Ethiopia), where, if you have permission, you can continue out of the country. It is possible to take short visits across the border, however, just to look around, at the nod of indulgent border guards. There is a military presence here, due to the fact that local Somalis have become restless in the past. (It is advisable to check the current situation before making any trip.)
The principal centre, **Isiolo**, in the southwest, is the gateway to the area on a good road from Nairobi. From here you can go on to **Wajir**, which is something of a surprise – a sizeable and busy settlement, with an air more Arab than African. It is surrounded by

THE NORTH AND EAST

wells, vital as a water supply to camel-herders, and there is a fortress.

◆◆◆
MARSABIT NATIONAL PARK
just outside Marsabit town
This is the principal draw in the northeast, thickly forested and mountainous. You can drive around flooded volcanic craters, the largest one called **Gof Bongole**. The park is famous for its long-tusked elephants, and has a vast and noisy bird life.
Open: all year; admission charge.

◆◆
SAMBURU NATIONAL RESERVE
north of Isiolo
A very beautiful park, this 116-square-mile (300 sq km) area takes in the Samburu National Reserve and the Buffalo Springs and Shaba National Reserves, situated around the Ewaso Nyiro River.
It has a damp climate and, besides scrubby savannahs, lots of riverside woods; so wildlife is viewable year-round. There are plenty of monkeys (the leopard's favourite food), and gerenuk can be seen here, as well as the diminutive dik-dik, with crocodile and ostrich adding to the list. Being lush riverine country, the forest is filled with fine trees, and the unusual branched palm, the doum, shakes its feathery head high over the bush, which you can now survey on balloon trips.
Down river, and to the east of Samburu is **Shaba**, a less visited national reserve. The name

means copper, but it's a misnomer, and the elephants you may see are merely red with earth dust. The reserve is still rated highly for its wildlife, but the accommodation is primitive, and if you stay over it will need to be in a tented camp, giving you a sense of being a bit closer to Africa.
These tracts of land, and the neighbouring **Isiolo Reserve**, border the earth-laden Ewaso Nyiro River to the north, which has its source in the Aberdare Range. Shaba was the home of Joy Adamson, and here the famous author raised a young leopard.
She was killed at Shaba in 1980, and her husband was later gunned down in the nearby **Kora** in 1989, during his unending war against poachers.

Accommodation
The only place to stay in the Marsabit National Park (apart from camping) is the well-sited **Marsabit Lodge**, close to the main gate.
Samburu Serena Lodge can be booked from Nairobi (tel: 339800), as can the **Buffalo Springs Lodge** (tel: 336858) and **Sarova Shaba Lodge** (tel: 333233).
Buffalo Springs National Reserve in the southerly section is a popular lodge; here there is a series of pools and damp, boggy marsh surrounds – magnets for animals, which can be viewed easily from the terrace. The other lodges are **Samburu Game Lodge** and **River Lodge**, to the west and on the edge of the park.

GAME PARKS

GAME PARKS

The main game parks are off the Nairobi-Mombasa axis; several of them can easily be reached from these cities, where there are many firms willing to plan your visit, be it a day or several, in luxury or simply 'back to nature'.

Packages can include all meals and accommodation, or you can self-cater with you own transport if you wish, using the usually well-organised campsites at the parks. Before doing this, you should check carefully the items you will need, from tin-openers to candles, sleeping bags to supplies of bottled water, matches to mosquito repellants. See that you have all you need, especially of vital supplies.

Some people want to see more than animals, and there are rich reserves of bird life in many parks, both dry and wet. All

Inherently lazy, lions are still powerful and effective hunters

sorts of plants, butterflies and insects are on hand, too, and some go specifically to find rare snakes and exotic lizards. The pursuit of such wildlife can often take you well away from camera-waving crowds in the little Volkswagen buses.

If you want to see Africa, you will not worry that you may take longer to get around the parks than perhaps anticipated. They are often larger than you expect, and the tracks are rough.

By far the best are such parks as **Amboseli**, the **Masai-Mara, Tsavo East** and **West, Meru, Mount Kenya**, the **Aberdare Range, Lake** Nakuru, **Shimba Hills, Mount Elgon, Marsabit** and **Samburu**. Most of these are described elsewhere in this book.

There are several National

Sweetwaters Camp
Wangu Embori Farm

GAME PARKS

Elephants: watch from a safe distance

Reserves (usually smaller), as distinct from National Parks, and these spaces, run by local councils and frequently close to official parks, should not be overlooked as possible quiet and worthwhile places.

◆◆
AMBOSELI NATIONAL PARK
off the Nairobi-Mombasa axis and close to the Tanzanian border

Some parks are more popular and accessible than others, and therefore more crowded. Amboseli has that problem, for, in addition to the animals, it also has the marvellous backdrop of Mount Kilimanjaro, a must for photographers and a scene often pictured in posters for Kenya's tourism (see also page 85).

◆◆
TAITA HILLS
near Voi, between the two Tsavo parks

This is not a national park, but a private reserve, the Taita Hills Game Sanctuary. The Hilton-run **Taita Hills Lodge** (tel: Muratate 44, or through Nairobi Hilton, 334000) is a nice old creeper-clad building, with lawns and a small park, where you may well spot lion, eland and elephant, as well as smaller animals such as jackals. Not far away is another Hilton place, the much photographed **Salt Lick Lodge** (tel: as above).

Here there is a rather bare water-hole, overlooked by rooms in toadstool-like constructions. You can sleep in a room on a stalk, and, if you wish, be woken at night when an unusual animal comes to drink.

It is peaceful here, but perhaps not eventful enough, although at night the spectacle of hundreds of bush babies' eyes shining can be quite magical. There is also a dank, subterranean chamber that will take you, by an underground passage, to the middle of the patch. From slit window-spaces you can view the game at very close quarters indeed, and this 'first hand' experience can be exciting.

The Taita Hills themselves are a very scenic area of dramatic mounds rising from the plains, densely thick with vegetation. There are twice-weekly market days at the principal and charming town, **Wundanyi**, which has some very agreeable bed and breakfast hotels. The scenery is surprising, viewed from narrow

Lodges are essential safari halts

roads twisting like snakes through the hills. After the plains and the dusty open country nearby, the weather is cool and the air fresh. This is altogether a surprising place, handy when you feel the need for a rest.

◆◆◆
TSAVO WEST
off the Nairobi–Mombasa road, to the southwest, at Tsavo town
This park, together with Tsavo East, across the highway and rail line, is one of the biggest anywhere. The two Tsavos are now believed to have a cycle of change as long as 40 years. Currently these dry areas are becoming greener. These enormous reserves are also the places where poaching has been much in evidence. You will find lots of wilderness but not too much wildlife in Tsavo East.

GAME PARKS

Tsavo West has a great deal more to offer. Its huge expanse of dry, rocky and dusty bush country is sometimes grim, yet never without an allure. Try a visit to the popular pools known as **Mzima Springs**, where, with luck, you will see hippos swimming from an underwater passage (see also page 93).

Accommodation
There are several lodges in Amboseli National Park, with the **Amboseli Serena Lodge**, just inside the park near a swamp (tel: 711077 in Nairobi) an attractive option. **Amboseli Lodge** (tel: 337510 in Nairobi) and **Kilimanjaro Safari Lodge** (tel: 337510 in Nairobi) are in the middle of the park.
The Hilton hotels, **Taita Hills Lodge** (tel: 334000 in Nairobi) and **Salt Lick Lodge** (tel: 334000 in Nairobi) are interesting options in Taita Hills. In Tsavo West, there is good viewing from the terraces of the **Kilaguni** and **Ngulia** (tel: 336858 in Nairobi for both lodges).

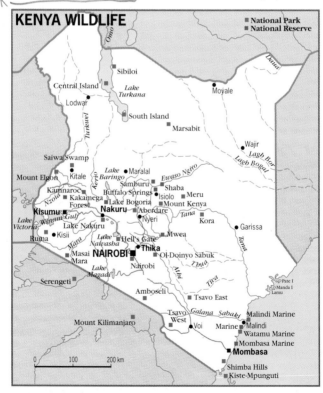

KENYA WILDLIFE

■ National Park
■ National Reserve

PEACE AND QUIET

Wildlife and Countryside in Kenya

by Paul Sterry

Gentle giants: despite their size, elephants are known for grace

For anyone whose imagination has been caught by wildlife films about the African bush, a visit to Kenya is like a dream come true. Despite natural and man-made problems that afflict the country and its wildlife, vast herds of wildebeest and zebra, sometimes hundreds of thousands strong, still wander the plains. Giraffes have been known to enter the outskirts of Nairobi, and within an hour's drive of the city centre, lions and cheetahs can be seen roaming free.

Tourism is Kenya's number one source of foreign revenue, with wildlife safaris featuring prominently among the attractions. It is not surprising, therefore, that a whole range of safaris and tours is now available, most involving visits to the game reserves and national parks for which Kenya is justly famous.

Some people choose to 'go it alone' and hire a jeep and head off into the bush. Although tremendously exciting, this can be a daunting prospect for the inexperienced traveller and it is often far better to use the knowledge and resources provided by organised safaris. Expensive trips are generally based around park lodges and offer most of the comforts of home, but for an authentic taste of the African bush, opt for a cheaper safari where camping is the only accommodation. To sit around a camp fire at night serenaded by baboons, hyaenas and lions is an unforgettable experience.

In common with many cities in developing nations, Nairobi has a surprising variety of wildlife living successfully alongside the human inhabitants. Roadside acacias, suburban gardens and even ornamental parks harbour birds and insects, while overhead the visitor will inevitably see flocks of black kites circling in search of food.

PEACE AND QUIET

The grounds of quieter hotels such as the Fairview offer birdwatchers the chance to become familiar with common African birds at close range. Olive thrushes and aptly named superb starlings probe the lawns for grubs, while variable sunbirds and Kikuyu white-eyes forage among the ornamental flowers, scarcely larger than the colourful butterflies alongside which they feed. The trees are full of birds: fiscal shrikes, speckled mousebirds, Reichenow's weavers, white-eyed slaty flycatchers and golden-rumped tinkerbirds are among those likely to be seen. The smaller parks and public gardens in the city are often planted with ornamental flowers such as bougainvillea. However, around Museum Hill and the nearby Nairobi River patches of original scrub still remain. Mountain wagtails and red-breasted wrynecks have been recorded in these areas, as have migrant birds such as common sandpiper, but more common species such as augur buzzard, African firefinch, bronze manakin and streaky seedeater are more likely. Nairobi City Park, situated near the Aga Khan Hospital, is by far the best place to observe wildlife within the boundaries of the city. Although essentially a recreational park, large tracts of the original hill forest, which once cloaked the area, still remain. The park's troops of Syke's monkeys are unafraid of people and fiscal shrikes and common bulbuls are similarly bold. Sadly, in recent years, attacks on visitors wandering Nairobis'

streets and parks have become frequent enough for a warning to have to be made here. Travelling alone can no longer be recommended and visitors should not carry valuables.

Nairobi National Park
Within half an hour's drive of the centre of Nairobi, the visitor can reach the boundaries of the city's own national park. Despite the close proximity of urban development, wildlife still thrives, and, with the exception of elephants, all the big game animals of Africa can usually be seen.
Within minutes of entering the park you will see small herds of wildebeest, zebra and impala. Cheetahs and lions are quite common but are generally difficult to see as they lie camouflaged in the dry grass.

Black rhinos
Widespread and often well organised poaching has decimated the black rhino population of East Africa. It is perhaps ironic, therefore, that one of the easiest places to see them is right on the doorstep of Kenya's capital. A small population has been established in Nairobi National Park where the presence of park guards and tourists affords them a degree of protection. Despite the comparatively small size of the park and bulk of these magnificent creatures, they can be remarkably difficult to locate. The rhinos are usually most active at dawn and dusk and are usually found well away from the park entrances in areas of lush grassland.

The chameleon exploits the art of camouflage for survival's sake

One of the sadder indictments of modern times is that the easiest way to see one of the big cats in the park is to watch for the dust-trails of converging Landrovers: once one vehicle finds its quarry, dozens soon descend on the scene.

Driving across the dry plains, you will often see groups of vultures gathered around the remains of a kill. These groups are generally made up of three or more species, with the large lappet-faced vulture taking precedence over white-backed and Ruppell's vultures.

On the flat landscape, ostriches are easy to see and groups of several birds are not uncommon. Because of their size, giraffes are similarly conspicuous as they browse the spiny acacia bushes, and lucky visitors may even see one of the black rhinos which have been introduced to the park. Coke's hartebeest, Thomson's gazelle and buffalo are more widespread, however, and the endearing

warthog is also a frequent sight. Visitors are allowed to walk freely along the banks of a stretch of the Athi River, although under the watchful eyes of armed guards. Huge Nile crocodiles and pink-skinned hippos bask in the pools, and an unusual bird, Peter's finfoot, is sometimes seen by quiet observers. The vegetation which fringes the river is home to terrapins, as well as such birds as malachite kingfishers, little bee-eaters and singing cisticolas.

Amboseli National Park

Close to the border with Tanzania and in the shadow of Mount Kilimanjaro, Amboseli is one of the best places in Kenya to see big game. The park has been badly hit by recent droughts and so, not surprisingly, the focal point of the park is Amboseli Lake, the size of which fluctuates greatly

PEACE AND QUIET

according to time of year and rainfall. At all times, however, the waters of the lake, together with the marshes which surround it, act like a magnet for the wildlife of the region. Accommodation within the park ranges from comfortable lodges to campsites which are little more than prescribed areas of bush. Around these, however, game animals such as buffalo, warthog and Thomson's gazelle are frequently seen and charming little birds called Taveta golden weavers are common. Elephants often wander through the campsites at night, but fortunately their great size belies their skill at avoiding guy-ropes and the tents themselves. So quiet are these gentle giants that their excursions often go unnoticed. Elephants are also commonly seen around the edges of the marshes, feeding on tree bark and foliage or cooling off in the mud. They often bathe in close

proximity to buffalo and the few remaining black rhino of the park, the latter having suffered greatly from poachers, and all three species are frequently accompanied by small groups of cattle egrets. These elegant, white birds catch animals disturbed by the large mammals and are sometimes seen riding on their backs. This habit of hitching a lift is also shared by oxpeckers which, in return for the ride, repay their host's generosity by picking off ticks and other parasites from the skin (for which they earned their name).

The marshes are also excellent for birds, crowned cranes, goliath herons, purple herons and squacco herons feed alongside three species of egret and the bizarre hammerkop, so-named because of its strangely shaped head. Black crakes,

Soda water: Lake Magadi's crust gives birds a safe margin

water dikkops, long-toed lapwings, blacksmith plovers and African jacanas are also common around the margins of the lake, while open water attracts flocks of pink-backed and white pelicans, Egyptian geese and white-backed duck. Smaller birds keep a wary eye open for African fish eagles, which perch on dead branches around the lake. They feed by skilfully plucking fish from the surface of the water but they are not averse to catching birds if they present an easy target. Amboseli also has good numbers of lions and cheetahs. Cheetahs in particular are invariably found on the dry, open plains which constitute most of the park's area and are often seen feeding on fresh kills of Thomson's gazelle.
Trails of dust from converging tourist trucks often indicate that a family group has been located and if the vehicles keep a respectful distance from the feeding cats, the animals appear oblivious to their presence and continue until they have had their fill. The dry acacia scrub is also the habitat of gerenuks, long-necked antelopes which often reach choice leaves and foliage by standing on their hind legs to gain extra height. Semi-desert birds are also common; among these, because of their size, the bustards are the most conspicuous species to be seen. Black-bellied, white-bellied and Hartlaub's bustards are often found, but the Kori bustard, which is the largest living bird capable of flight, is by far the most spectacular.

Lake Magadi

On Kenya's border with Tanzania and an easy day's journey from Nairobi, Lake Magadi is set in the great Rift Valley and like other lakes in the Valley is alkaline, with a 'skin' of soda. The soda 'skin' or crust gives excellent protection to the birds, since it collapses as soon as anything attempts to stand on it – so beware. The shallow waters are beloved of water birds such as flamingos, pelicans, herons and spoonbills, while the margins are the haunt of a wide variety of wading birds. Even the surrounding bush has its share of interesting wildlife and the drive south from the capital is normally rewarded with exciting views of game animals and bush birds.
Despite the proximity of water, many of the mammals and birds avoid the lake itself for much of the time and are superbly adapted to the arid conditions. For example, larks search the dry soil for seeds and insects and parties of ostriches somehow find enough to eat. Like the ostriches, gerenuks also prefer this dry habitat and are often seen standing on their hind legs to reach a choice morsel of vegetation, but zebras, wildebeests, hartebeests and giraffes stay closer to the lake itself. At dawn, many of the animals will come to the water's edge to drink and, not surprisingly, this is also when their main predators, lion and cheetah, are most easily seen. The lake itself is often thronged with flamingos, with lesser usually outnumbering greater

flamingo. Flocks are often patchily distributed around the lake, where feeding conditions happen to be best, and among their numbers will be both white and pink-backed pelicans and African spoonbills as well as smaller numbers of egrets and grey and goliath herons.

Migrant and resident waders feed around the margins, with long-legged, black-winged stilts mingling with avocets and ruff, while chestnut-banded sandplovers chase along the shoreline in search of insects. Although comparatively easy to see at Lake Magadi, these delightful little birds are found nowhere else in Kenya.

Aberdare National Park
Set in the Aberdare Mountains in Kenya's central highlands, the Aberdare National Park is one of the most beautiful regions in the whole of East Africa and is less than a day's journey from Nairobi. With most of the park lying above 10,000 feet (3,000m), the cloud forest and high altitude moorland which make up the park are often shrouded in mist but this only adds to the romance of the Aberdares: memories of elephants emerging from the swirling mist will be slow to fade.

In the eastern sector of the park is Treetops Hotel, famous the world over not only for its wildlife and hospitality but also for its distinguished guests: royalty, politicians and film stars have all stayed here.

Water-holes are conveniently sited for veranda-viewing and among the creatures attracted to drink, elephants, giant forest hogs, buffaloes, impalas, birds of prey and crowned cranes are regularly encountered.

After dark, the illuminations may reveal nightjars hunting for insects, as well as hyaenas, genets or even a rare glimpse of an elusive leopard.

In the bush surrounding Treetops, troops of olive baboons, Syke's monkey and black-faced vervet are found, often screaming in alarm at the presence of an intruder in their territory. Birds, too, are numerous and several species of bee-eater, kingfisher, roller and hornbill can be seen on even a short drive. A careful search of the foliage will reveal sunbirds such as amethyst and variable sunbirds, golden-rumped tinkerbirds, chin-spot flycatchers and speckled mousebirds, as well as a wide variety of Eurasian migrants from October to February.

The higher elevations of the park are dominated by moorland vegetation with bamboo finally grading into giant heath and tussock grass at the highest levels. The open terrain makes wildlife observation easier than in the forests on the lower slopes: duikers, eland and civet are seen regularly and there is even a chance of a black rhino or of the elusive antelope called the bongo. The flowering bushes attract a variety of birdlife, the most noticeable being the scarlet-tufted malachite sunbird, seldom found at lower elevations.

> **Nakurus' Fickle Flamingos**
> Lake Nakuru is justly famous for its flamingos. Both greater and lesser flamingos are found here, and on occasions over two million birds congregate, spreading evenly around the edge of the lake. For the best impression of the sheer numbers, Baboon Rocks, on the west side of Nakuru, gives a bird's-eye view. Because of its elevation, Baboon Rocks is also a good spot for watching birds of prey. Visitors should note that water conditions, and hence feeding, at Lake Nakuru can change from month to month. Sometimes the flamingos will abandon the lake altogether until good feeding returns. However, if not here they will generally only have moved to Lake Bogoria further up the Rift Valley.

Lake Nakuru National Park

As dawn breaks over Lake Nakuru, the early-rising visitor is treated to one of the most amazing natural spectacles to be seen anywhere on earth. Mist rising from the Lake's surface is caught by the first rays of sunlight and as the light intensity increases, phenomenal numbers of flamingos, pelicans and many other water birds are highlighted in the orange glow. Such is the density of water birds that you are unlikely to see such a concentration of wildlife anywhere else.

Many people stay at the campsites on the northwest side of the lake. Fiscal shrikes and arrow-marked babblers feed around the tents, which are often the subject of the unwelcome attention of vervet monkeys.

From here it is a short walk or drive to the edge of the lake, where close views may be had of flamingos, white and pink-backed pelicans, black-winged stilts, egrets and yellow-billed storks. The muddy margins of this alkaline lake often preserve the footprints of hippos which emerge at night to feed on the surrounding vegetation. Also littering the edge of the lake are vast quantities of feathers, droppings and the remains of dead birds. Not surprisingly, therefore, scavengers have a field day and chief among these at Nakuru are the marabou storks. Standing nearly as tall as a man, these birds loaf around in small groups, their bald necks and dirty bills giving them a most unsavoury appearance. A road leads south along the west side of the lake and even on a short drive you will see a wide variety of game animals. Defassa waterbuck browse in the bush, the males often pausing to scent-mark twigs with the musk glands near their eyes. Giraffe, Burchell's zebra, impala and Thomson's gazelle are also comparatively easy to see, while the tiny Kirk's dik-dik hides among the tangled bush vegetation.

In places, the track on the west side of the lake passes close to the water's edge, making photography easy. Great and little egrets, African spoonbills, Egyptian geese, grey-headed gulls and sacred ibises can all be seen and, from September until March, European and Asian waders spend the winter here. Marsh and wood sandpipers, ruff and little stint feed alongside resident three-banded plovers and blacksmith plovers and large flocks of whiskered, white-winged black and gull-billed terns hawk the air for insects. At one point, the road passes close to an abandoned nest site of greater flamingos: thousands of mud platforms dot the lake margin, each one at a regular distance from its neighbours.

Lake Naivasha

Lying mid-way between Nairobi and Lake Nakuru, Lake Naivasha is one of Kenya's best-known Rift Valley lakes. Since the capital is comparatively close, the lake could be visited on a day trip, but in order to get the most from Naivasha a longer stay is recommended. For anyone particularly interested in water birds, Lake Naivasha is outstanding, but for those with a more general interest, there is also a wide range of game animals to be found around its margins.

Like the neighbouring Nakuru, Naivasha hosts greater and lesser flamingos but since these extraordinary birds have very precise feeding requirements, which Naivasha sometimes fails to meet, there are times when the lake is entirely devoid of both species. However, even if flamingos are absent, there will be no shortage of other water birds to be seen. Purple herons and their immense relatives, the aptly named goliath herons, stand patiently around the margins, while great and little egrets and squacco herons are more active in their pursuit of prey.

The waters teem with fish,

amphibians and invertebrates and these form the exclusive diet of many of the birds. African darters, cormorants and white and pink-backed pelicans patrol the open water, while around the margins malachite, pied, giant and pygmy kingfishers perch and scan the water below for fish. Patches of water lily provide an ideal habitat for African jacanas, crested coots, purple gallinules and black crakes, the latter keeping a wary eye open for patrolling African fish eagles. The diet of these immense birds is not confined to fish – unsuspecting small birds and reptiles often fall victim.

In the bush country surrounding Lake Naivasha, zebras, giraffes, Coke's hartebeests, impalas and bushbucks are often seen, and the foliage of acacia trees is good for birds. Several species of cuckoo, sunbird, weaver and woodpecker may be found and the elusive red-breasted wryneck is also regularly reported. By way of contrast, at nearby Hell's Gate there are immense eroded cliffs which offer a different range of birds. Although having something of a reputation as bandit country, the cliffs are well worth visiting, especially for the Verreaux's eagles, lammergeiers, and vultures that might be seen drifting on the thermals.

Lake Baringo and Lake Bogoria National Reserve

The great Rift Valley of East Africa runs the length of Kenya like an immense scar and is a testament to the forces of nature at work beneath the earth's

PEACE AND QUIET

Bandit and bird country – Hell's Gate

surface. The huge valley floor is a natural place for water to collect and so, not surprisingly, the country's most famous lakes, including Magadi, Naivasha and Nakuru, are found here. Continuing the chain northward, lakes Bogoria and Baringo complete the sequence in central Kenya and offer a wide variety of wildlife to the intrepid visitor.

Along its length, the Rift Valley is fringed by volcanic activity. Mount Kenya and Mount Kilimanjaro are the two most spectacular examples of this, but at Lake Bogoria, hot springs are another manifestation of geothermal activity below the earth's crust. The influence that this activity has upon the water, both in terms of its chemistry and its temperature, does not favour all animal life, but flamingos frequently find the water conditions exactly to their liking. The sight of thousands of these pale pink birds feeding through the dawn mists of Bogoria is a memorable one. Around the edges of both Bogoria and Baringo, black-winged stilts and avocets feed

on small aquatic animals, their numbers boosted from September until March by migrants from Europe and Asia such as ruff, marsh sandpipers and little stints. Whiskered, white-winged black and gull-billed terns may be seen throughout the year, but again migrants escaping the northern winter cause a dramatic increase in numbers. African spoonbills, little and great egrets, yellow-billed storks and Goliath herons also make use of the aquatic bonanza and marabou storks wait patiently for any left-over scraps.

In the bush which surrounds the lakes, impalas, zebras and wildebeests can be found in reasonable numbers. Little and white-fronted bee-eaters, lilac-breasted rollers and fiscal shrikes use low bushes as look-out perches, while the canopy of larger acacia trees harbours a variety of weavers, flycatchers, honey-guides and orioles, as well as interesting species such as silverbird and curl-crested helmet shrike.

PEACE AND QUIET

Masai-Mara National Reserve

The Masai-Mara is *the* place to visit if you want to see huge numbers of animals as well as variety. Within the vast boundaries of the reserve, part of which is managed strictly like a national park and part of which is used by tribal Masai, huge herds of wildebeest and zebra still roam, together with their attendant predators and scavengers. Part of the reason for the thriving populations is that the park's southwest border adjoins the Serengeti National Park in Tanzania and the herds migrate between the two sites, following the rains and fresh growth of grass.

Fortunately for them, the herds of migrating wildebeest, zebra and topi do not recognise frontiers between countries and are not hindered by them. However, natural barriers such as the Mara River represent a real obstacle to their travels and their crossing is a spectacle many visitors try to witness. The crossing points are sites which have been used by generations of animals and are the places where the water is shallow and banks easy to climb. However, they are still justifiably wary of entering the murky water and with good reason: Nile crocodiles lurk there and predators such as lions or hyaenas may wait to pick off exhausted animals on the other side.

Elsewhere along its course, the Mara River is the haunt of hippos which wallow in the water and sometimes sunbathe. This activity is performed with a degree of caution, however, since hippos have a delicate skin which burns easily. Nile crocodiles also bask along the banks and little bee-eaters and brown-hooded kingfishers perch on overhanging branches.

Hyaenas dine near the Mara River

Despite the seasonal migrations of many of the game animals, large herds of wildebeest and zebra, with smaller numbers of impala, topi, water buffalo and hartebeest, can be seen at any time of year. Benefiting from this abundance of food, the density of lions in the Masai-Mara is one of the highest in Africa. Leopards are also regularly reported. The latter are surely the most elegant of the big cats, and although usually secretive they are occasionally found sleeping in the branches of

The family life of lions
These days, in the more populated southern parts of Kenya, lions are more-or-less restricted to living within the boundaries of national parks and reserves. Although most such sites, including even Nairobi National Park, have these big cats, one of the best places to see them in their true bush setting is in the Masai Mara. Several large prides live here, each dominated by a large-maned male. Although full grown but immature males are tolerated within the group, the pride is made up largely of mature females and their cubs. Females are responsible for almost all the hunting activity of the pride, which takes place mostly at dawn and dusk. Most safari visitors look for, and find, the prides resting up in the shade of the bush during the middle of the day at which time they seem idle and relaxed. Go on a bush run at dawn and it will be a different matter. Cute and playful lions will have been transformed into the efficient and powerful killers they truly are.

acacias during the heat of the day.
Because of their size, elephants and giraffes are difficult to miss among the scrub, but the diminuitive dik-dik, a tiny antelope, requires a keen eye to spot it. They are justifiably alert and wary since packs of hyaenas commonly roam the Masai-Mara and are sometimes seen lying up in the heat of the day.
The open plains, which are the realm of the great herds of game animals, are also full of birds. Lilac-breasted rollers, fiscal shrikes and birds of prey perch on low bushes, while yellow-throated longclaws and flocks of Hildebrandt's starlings forage for insects on the ground below. Marshy areas attract wading birds and herons, which are dwarfed by the immense saddle-billed stork.

Tsavo National Park
Tsavo is Kenya's largest wildlife wilderness and much of it is completely inaccessible to visitors. Although many of Kenya's national parks are seriously threatened by encroaching human activity, this is not true of Tsavo: the area covered by the two separate parks, **East** and **West**, is so vast and the land so rugged and harsh that most of it is untouched African 'bush'. The animals are often much harder to see than in areas like the Masai-Mara or Amboseli but the setting of red soils (which often stain the hides of the game animals), stately baobab trees and the volcanic cones more than makes up for this.

PEACE AND QUIET

Elephants and giraffes are surprisingly difficult to spot in this landscape, although sooner or later the visitor is sure to encounter them. Zebras and impalas wander through the scrub and observers may also see oryx, steinbok or dik-dik.

While driving through the park, troops of olive baboons will sometimes slow your progress as they cross the road. They will often visit campsites within the park – when they rapidly lose their interest value and become a nuisance. The roadside vegetation also provides perches for a variety of birds, including white-headed buffalo weaver, pygmy falcon, lilac-breasted and rufous-crowned roller as well as several species of hornbills.

Camping is the best way to enjoy Tsavo, but that does not mean that the hospitality of the lodges, in the form of cool drinks and swimming pools, need be ignored. Wildlife also finds a refuge around these lodges: at Kilaguni, for example, you can sit quietly, glass in hand, watching d'Arnaud's barbet and red-billed hornbill at close range, while zebra and wildebeest drink from the man-made water-holes below the veranda.

The volcano and lava flows around Mount Shetani bear witness to the forces of nature pent-up beneath the surface of the land. This is a harsh and arid part of the park, but for contrast visit Mzima Springs. Unlike many African rivers, the waters are crystal clear and an underwater observatory allows close-up views of swimming hippos. Lush waterside vegetation harbours green heron and several species of cisticola; the lucky observer may even see Peter's finfoot swimming low in the water.

Mount Kenya National Park

Kenya is a country of contrasting habitats and nowhere demonstrates the extremes better than Mount Kenya National Park, which lies more or less on the Equator. Within the boundaries of the park, much of which is cloaked in virgin forest and lies above 11,000 feet (3,300m), are the twin peaks of Batian and Nelion, which rise to over 17,000 feet (5,000m) above sea level. Considering the altitude, it is perhaps not surprising to find permanent snow and ice fields here, but the sight of elephants and rhino roaming the lower slopes of the mountain makes this park one of the most memorable in the whole of Kenya.

The point of access to the park for most people is the Sirimon Track, which departs from the main road near Nanyuki. The drives takes you through forested lower slopes, which are the haunt of woodland birds such as red-headed parrot, Hartlaub's turaco, silvery-cheeked hornbill, olive pigeon and Ayre's hawk-eagle. Mammals, although comparatively difficult to see, include buffalo, elephant, black rhino, bushbuck, bongo and giant forest hog. There is even a chance of seeing leopard although, as elsewhere in

Kenya, these beautiful cats are shy and elusive.

As the drive continues, the forests become more open and gradually merge with bamboo and finally, at the highest altitudes, with 'forests' of *Hypericum* and the Afro-Alpine 'moorland' for which Mount Kenya is famous. This extraordinary landscape is dominated by giant species of heaths, *Lobelia* and *Senecio*, all of which have more familiar, and much smaller, counterparts growing wild elsewhere in the world and in cultivation. The plants here, however, have adapted to one of the harshest environments on earth: daytime temperatures and ultra-violet radiation can be fierce, due to the overhead sun and thin atmosphere, while at night temperatures fall close to freezing point.

At high altitudes, parties of alpine swifts can be seen hawking the air for insects, while birds of prey soar overhead. Scarlet-tufted malachite

sunbirds are a speciality of the high moorland, feeding on the nectar provided by flowering plants, while mountain chats use the larger spikes as convenient perches.

Marsabit National Reserve

The comparative isolation of Marsabit from Nairobi means that fewer tourists visit this park than most others; the drive from the capital is a long one and the terrain is really suitable only for four-wheel drive vehicles. However, those adventurous visitors who do manage the journey will find good numbers of widespread game animals as well as several more unusual species set amid spectacular scenery: dense forests cloak the hillsides and volcanoes and barren lava fields add contrast to the varied terrain.

The reticulated giraffes which haunt the forested slopes are perhaps the most impressive

The elegant Grant's gazelle

PEACE AND QUIET

mammals of Marsabit. The patterns on their chestnut coats, divided into blocks of colour by fine white lines, look as if they have been skilfully painted. Swamps and water-holes near the Marsabit Lodge act like a magnet for many of the animals of the surrounding bush and offer good chances of seeing one of Marsabit's other mammal specialities, the greater kudu, an antelope distinguished from its lesser relative by the larger, spiral horns and fringed throat. Most of Kenya's other dry-country game animals can also be found including elephant, Beisa oryx, gerenuk, buffalo and Grant's gazelle, as well as the beautifully marked Grevy's zebra.

In addition to the game animals, the supplies of water at Marsabit Lodge and Lake Paradise also attract birds such as waders, herons, storks, kingfishers and birds of prey; exactly which species are present depends upon the time of year and the water level. Several species of sandgrouse pay brief visits at dawn or dusk, while ostriches, cream-coloured coursers, Namaqua doves and Heuglin's bustards prefer the dry country and approach water less frequently.

Meru National Park

Meru first shot to public attention as the location for the late Joy Adamson's studies of lions and as the home of her most famous subject, the lioness Elsa. Elsa's descendants survive in the reserve to this day, along with a wealth of other animals, making a safari to Meru a

On safari – Samburu National Reserve

memorable experience. Unlike many of Kenya's national parks, Meru comprises a range of different habitats which encourages diversity in the animals and plants found there. The rivers which dissect the reserve are the haunt of hippos, herons and the elusive Peter's finfoot and are lined with statuesque palms and riverine forest, while on land the vegetation ranges from *Combretum* bush and acacia or palm woodland to tropical forest.

The game animals roam widely throughout Meru, their exact location determined by recent rainfall, time of day and time of year. However, a day's drive through the bush should produce good views of both Grevy's and common (or Burchell's) zebra, reticulated giraffe, hartebeest, warthog, elephant, kongoni, Beisa oryx and lesser kudu.

Acacia woodland can often appear lifeless at first but wait, look and listen beneath the boughs and you will be rewarded: pearl-spotted owlets and Verreaux's eagle owls sit quietly in the branches while grey-backed cameropteras and white-winged scrub robins forage secretively near to the ground. Colourful barbets, violet wood-hoopoes, little bee-eaters, yellow-billed and Von der Decken's hornbills soon become apparent and many smaller bird species rove around in mixed flocks. Sooner or later you should encounter a group which may include orioles, flycatchers, black-headed bush-shrikes, tropical boubous, straight-crested helmet shrikes and northern brubru.

As a reminder of the frailty of even the toughest-seeming of Africa's wildlife, Meru was, until late in 1989, the only place in Kenya where you could see white rhinos. The small herd, guarded night and day, was wiped out one night by poachers armed with machine guns. They sawed the animals' horns off with chainsaws and escaped.

Samburu National Reserve

Samburu and adjacent Buffalo Springs National Reserves, with their wild and scenic terrain, form the southernmost and most easily accessible part of Kenya's northern territories. The blend of birds and mammals is subtly different from national parks in the south of the country and many are species more at home on the Ethiopian border. The water-holes, and more especially Buffalo Springs and the Ewaso Nyiro River, act as

magnets for the wildlife of the surrounding bush. Fortunately, the campsites and Samburu Lodge are close to the river and afford almost unlimited scope for safari visitors. Nile crocodiles and hippos can sometimes be seen sunbathing on the banks in the morning; the heat of the midday is generally too much for both species and they retreat into the cooling water.

Many of the bush birds and mammals visit Buffalo Springs and the river at dawn or dusk to drink. Long lines of vulturine and tufted guinea-fowl and flocks of sandgrouse make their way to the water's edge, and buffalos, bushbucks, common waterbucks, impalas, warthogs and sometimes even elephants or black rhinos can be seen. During the day, a short drive through the bush will soon offer views of other game animals. Beisa oryx, easily recognised by their long, almost straight horns, blend in with the dry vegetation, and Grant's gazelle and gerenuk are also frequently seen. Both the common zebra and Grevy's zebra occur in Samburu, the narrow black markings on the latter making it one of Kenya's most elegant game animals, possibly only rivalled by the reticulated giraffes with which they are sometimes seen. Predators in Samburu include lion, cheetah, leopard and spotted hyaena, but it requires both luck and persistence to see them. Ground-feeding birds seen beside the tracks may include red-winged and fawn-coloured larks, yellow-throated longclaw, mourning and Namaqua doves, two-banded and Temminck's coursers and sandgrouse, ever-watchful of the skies above for birds of prey such as martial eagle, bateleur and tawny eagle. Because of their greater size, Kori and buff-crested bustards and ostriches are less prone to attack from the air but are still wary of potential ground predators. Ostriches in Samburu are represented by the Somali race of the species which is more elegantly marked than its counterpart, found in southern Kenya.

Lake Turkana

The Turkana region of northern Kenya is some of the most inhospitable terrain in the whole country. However, in the middle of this arid semi-desert lies Lake Turkana, formerly known as Lake Rudolf, which is both a haven for water birds and Nile crocodiles and an oasis for animals of the surrounding bush. The rugged terrain, rough roads and great distance from Nairobi mean that it is perhaps the least visited region in Kenya, but for those who make the effort it is a land of real adventure.

The region is best explored from camps either at the safari lodge on the southeast edge of the lake or the angling lodge on the west. In the scrub adjacent to the lake, Abyssinian ground hornbills plod around, looking dignified in their all-black plumage, and Abyssinian rollers and carmine bee-eaters can be seen perched on prominent branches. Flocks of flamingos may be encountered anywhere around the shore or more reliably in the crater lakes of Central Island. Many species of herons and egrets can also be found throughout the year and birds of prey and scavengers are never far away.

Lake Turkana is not only important to the wildlife of the surrounding bush; it is also of strategic importance to migrant birds from northern Europe and Asia. Hundreds of thousands pass through the region in March and April and again in September and October. Land birds such as wagtails and swallows are often encountered, but it is the wading birds that really attract the eye. Flocks of long-distance migrants such as spotted redshank and black-tailed godwit mingle with black-winged stilts and avocets, some of which breed more locally. Terns also pass through the region and flocks of whiskered and white-winged black terns skim through the air, sometimes mixing with resident Caspian terns.

Some areas of shoreline have breeding colonies of African skimmers, extraordinary birds whose bills have a lower mandible considerably longer than its upper counterpart. This apparently strange adaptation can sometimes be seen in action over the waters of the lake. As their name implies, skimmers 'skim' the water's surface with their lower mandible, just leaving a ripple; if it touches a fish, the upper mandible snaps shut, catching the prey. After an unsuccessful trawl, the birds often retrace their course because fish are sometimes attracted to the initial disturbance.

Gedi National Monument and Arabuko Sokoke Forest

Gedi National Monument, 12 miles (19km) south of Malindi on the Kenyan coast, protects the remains of a ruined Islamic city which dates back to the 13th century (see also pages 54–5). The city and the surrounding land appear to have been abandoned suddenly, for reasons which are still unknown, and forest soon regained its foothold.

Although parts of the site have been cleared of vegetation to allow public access, trails lead off into pristine forest which is very similar to nearby Arabuko Sokoke Forest. These two areas form some of the last patches of coastal tropical forest to be found on this stretch of East Africa and are host to an extraordinary range of animals. The roads leading to Gedi are largely flanked by agricultural land and cleared of virgin forest. However, overhead wires and dead branches provide perches for birds such as the Zanzibar sombre greenbul, a dull bird with a

Wildebeest and zebra make their way across the Mara River

beautiful song, Indian house crows, striped swallows and lilac-breasted rollers. Once under the canopy of the forest surrounding Gedi itself, the welcome shade is several degrees cooler than the surrounding countryside. Having studied the fascinating ruins, which abound with geckos and are the nest-site for mottled-throated spinetails, try following one of the forest trails which lead away from the buildings. Snakes, including the deadly black mamba, are sometimes seen, as is an extraordinary mammal known as yellow-rumped elephant shrew, an insectivorous shrew-like creature which may reach 18 inches (46cm) in length. Mammals and snakes are comparatively difficult to spot on the dappled forest floor but the visitor should have no difficulty in seeing the giant millipedes and giant African land snails which glide over the fallen leaves.

PEACE AND QUIET

Arabuko Sokoke Forest

stretches south from Gedi, parallel to the coast on the inland side of the main coast road. Several (unmarked) tracks lead into the forest and should be followed in order to avoid getting lost. As with the forests around Gedi, early morning provides the best opportunity for the naturalist: shy mammals like elephant shrews and duikers venture across the tracks and forest birds such as African pitta, green pigeon, Narina's trogon and southern banded harrier eagle may be seen.

Watamu Marine National Park and Mida Creek

Many people come to the Kenyan coast simply to enjoy the white, sandy beaches and warm seas, but turn your attention to the seashore and adjacent coastal land and you will soon find a wealth of wildlife. Some of the best areas lie between Mombasa and Malindi, and Watamu and adjacent Malindi Marine National Parks have been established to protect the finest stretches of coastline, coral reefs and mangroves.

Coral reefs are fascinating places and the dazzling array of marine life at Watamu will thrill first-time visitors and merit subsequent return trips. Although scuba-diving or glass-bottomed boats give the best views of the reef, even the simplest snorkel and mask will reveal an array of multi-coloured fish, corals and molluscs at low tide. Coral reefs are hard and jagged so

remember to wear plimsolls to protect your feet. You should also be well aware of the state of the tide since the waves can rise over the reef with surprising speed.

Waders, gulls and herons can be seen scavenging the remains of animals and plants along the tideline, but for variety and numbers, nearby Mida Creek should be visited. Almost landlocked, this shallow basin empties out at low tide to reveal vast mudflats which become covered with little stints, curlew sandpipers, sanderlings, greenshank, whimbrel, great and lesser sandplovers and crab plovers. The latter are seldom seen elsewhere in Kenya and their black and white plumage and immense bill make them easy to identify.

As the tide rises, huge flocks of waders take to the air, wheeling and turning in perfect synchrony. The mangrove-lined shores nearest the main coast road and on the northern side of the mouth of Mida Creek offer the best opportunities for viewing the mudflats and the mangroves themselves make a fascinating diversion from the birds.

Marine molluscs, mudskippers and fiddler crabs find the tangled roots and branches a safe sanctuary from the prying eyes of predatory birds.

Malindi

To the north of the coastal resort of Malindi lie amazing sandy beaches and dunes which stretch for several miles to the mouth of the Sokoke River. Since most holidaymakers do not venture far from the town itself, much of the area is completely undisturbed and a walk along the beach or through the golf course will lead to unspoilt areas full of wildlife.

The small-holdings and arable land on the edge of Malindi are favoured by lilac-breasted rollers, black cuckoos and Indian house crows, while overhead, parties of African palm swifts hawk for insects. As you reach the golf course, however, the bird life changes and sacred ibises and black headed plovers can be seen on the links, especially early in the morning.

Beyond the golf course lie the sand dunes, which are of far greater interest to the naturalist. Pools of water collect in some of the dune slacks and are favoured bathing and feeding sites for birds such as African spoonbill, African skimmer, openbill stork, black-winged stilt, greater and lesser sandplover and many other shorebirds. Large flocks of migrant Madagascar pratincoles roost among the dunes in August; and later in the year parties of carmine bee-eaters glide through the air.

Towards the mouth of the river, vast areas of mudflat are exposed at low tide. The wind often drifts dry sand onto areas of the mud, which can prove treacherous if stepped upon. Exercise caution when walking near to the water's edge. Vast numbers of waders and egrets feed on the marine life harboured by the mud and birds roost on exposed sandbanks. At least seven species of tern, including Caspian and crested terns, are regularly seen, and sooty and white-eyed gulls are also to be found.

At the mouth of the Sokoke River, mangroves have begun to colonise the mud and their tangled roots are full of invertebrate animals. Fiddler crabs with colourful pincers, ghost crabs and mudskippers are the most obvious residents, but a closer inspection of the mud will reveal thousands of marine molluscs.

Kakamega Forest National Reserve

Lying to the north of Lake Victoria, Kakamega Forest is all that remains of the extensive woodland which once cloaked the region. Rainfall is high here, and Kakamega has many of the species more usually associated with West African tropical forest. Encroached on all sides by small-holdings and farmland, Kakamega Forest is an exciting contrast to the rest of Kenya and a last refuge for many species found nowhere else in the country.

Over the years, human disturbance and hunting have driven out or exterminated many of the larger mammals, but most visitors should have no problem seeing black-and-white colobus and Syke's monkeys. Although the inquisitive nature of the latter species may at first be endearing, it can soon become

PEACE AND QUIET

annoying as they have been known to raid tents and visitors' bags. For the sake of the animals, please do not encourage them with food. In common with forests the world over, birdwatching in Kakamega is best at dawn when the birds are at their most active and vocal. Inevitably you will hear far more than you see, but the rewards of patient and persistent viewing will be well worthwhile. Whether or not birds are in view, forest glades and clearings will be full of insect life and the leaf litter on the forest floor will rustle with lizards and perhaps an elephant shrew. Visitors should also take time to watch the woodland floor for another, less benign, resident: the puff adder.

The Chyulu Hills

The Chyulu Hills lie to the south of the main road from Nairobi to Mombasa and rise to an elevation of over 9,000 feet (2,700m) above sea level, looking down on the surrounding plains. The area is not a national park or a game reserve and consequently human disturbance has reduced or eliminated the herds of larger game animals.
As you ascend the lower slopes, the dirt tracks pass through bush country where the occasional dik-dik is startled into action. Small groups of impala and oryx may also be seen, while solitary secretary birds patrol the grassland in search of prey.
These extraordinary birds were so-named because the

> **Sunbirds**
> Beside tracks and on the edges of patches of woodland and scrub, flowers grow in profusion and the colourful trumpets of *Leonotis* are a rich source of nectar for insects as well as for a specialised group of birds. Wait beside a patch of Leonotis for a short while and you are likley to see Sunbirds. These are attractive little birds of which many species have long, down-curved bills. Although they lack the ability to hover, they are in many other respects the African equivalent of South American hummingbirds. The bill is used to probe the flowers and several species, such as Tacazze, olive, variable and golden-winged sunbirds, may be seen in the same patch of flowers at the same time.

plumes on their heads reminded the first explorers of Victorian secretaries with quills behind their ears. Their long legs not only give them stature but allow them to tackle with impunity the venomous snakes which form a large part of their diet.
Because of the altitude, dawn over the Chyulu Hills is often a time of rolling mists and, although they are almost on the Equator, early morning temperatures can be decidedly chilly. However, the sun soon burns off the last remnants of cloud on most days and these early hours are the best time to see the birds since most species are actively feeding. Red-billed hornbill, white-browed coucal, fiscal shrike and black cuckoo-shrike can all be found,

although patience is often needed with species that feed among the foliage.

A Plea for Kenya's Wildlife

Kenya has a rich and varied wildlife heritage and one which attracts visitors from all over the world. So important is this resource that the income generated by safari tourists is a major fund of foreign revenue. However, there is another, less savoury source of foreign money which unless halted will, in the long term, have a profoundly adverse effect both on Kenya's wildlife and its tourist industry. This is the illegal trade in animals and animal products, which ranges from the capture of bustards for export as falconry quarry to the senseless slaughter of rhinos and elephants for ivory. So serious is the latter problem that some experts believe that the African elephant, together with both black and white rhinos, could be driven to extinction in the wild in the next 20 years unless poaching is stopped.

The Kenyan government now treats the problem with great seriousness: a shoot-to-kill policy is operated against ivory poachers, and most animal products and derivatives, including skins, carved horn and shells, are now banned from being exported. The Kenyan authorities have taken drastic action, but what can you, the visitor, do to help? Principally, condemn the ivory trade at every available opportunity and never be tempted to buy animals, or animal products, unless you are certain that their origins are legitimate. Never buy ivory, no matter what the source is said to be; at present there are just too many loopholes that enable dealers to flout international regulations designed to stop the use of ivory products.

Comparing notes: secretary birds, named for their quill-like plumes

FOOD AND DRINK

You will have to watch your stomach in Kenya, since local food and drink may not suit you. If in doubt, stick to hotel fare – in the big resorts it has been Westernised, and bland international dishes are available at hotels and in major towns. However, the local African fare can be both delicious and nutritious. By and large it will not be complicated, tending towards the plain yet spicy.

Take your pick of exotic drinks

Food

So much is dependent on what is locally available, and restaurants reflect this. There is plenty of fish along the coasts; meat is readily available inland, and lots of unusual vegetables and fruits. Be adventurous: try them.

Fruits are used in cooking (banana, coconut, apple) as well as in refreshing fruit salads featuring mango, papaya, pineapple, citrus and soft fruits. You can also try exotics that you won't see at home. Yams, plantains and breadfruits appear prepared in a variety of ways, often using spices and Indian influences. You will also find potato and root vegetables.

Maize is widely eaten; you can buy roasted cobs at street corners, and maize also forms the base of a porridge.

Rice, cooked in several ways, is a staple accompaniment to most dishes. Hot and strong sauces accompany some foods, with local hot peppers and spices being much enjoyed. Ask about these before you order.

Lentils, peas, beans and other pulses, both fresh and dried, are much used, and there are lots of salad vegetables, but vegetarians may have a problem finding meat or fishless dishes, since so much meat fat is used in cooking.

Meat (including game), is often served plain and grilled, as is fish, but there can also be curries and stews, and fish and crab with peppery sauces is a favourite. Remember when eating uncooked produce that it may have been washed in local water from polluted sources, and can cause acute digestion problems.

Outside the main cities you may have to 'be a local' whether you wish it or not, since eating places will often be simple. Eating at small cafés and neighbourhood restaurants (*hotelis*) can be most novel, as long as you take care and ensure that what you eat will not upset your stomach. In parts of the country away from the cities you will find local foods of Ethiopian, Somali and other origins. City offerings, particularly in Nairobi and Mombasa, can vary from Italian and Chinese to fish and chips.

Beverages

There are opportunities to try local brews such as Kenyan beers (available in all bars, cheap and thirst-quenching), and the soft drinks are good and cheap. Locally produced cordials such as passion fruit, pineapple, lime, orange, etc, make refreshing drinks, but ice is made with local water, so avoid it. Drink only bottled water.

Palm wine can be sampled cheaply around Mombasa – a powerful drink, served luke-warm in local bars. Mixed drinks in bars come in good portions; imported spirits and liqueurs are not cheap, but locally produced rum is a bargain.

Wines are not very good, although there is one made from papaya that you might want to try for interest. Imported wines can be found in a limited array, but they will be expensive.

Kenya grows its own coffee in vast estates, but you will often be given instant in cafés. Tea, or *chai*, is an odd, strong brew and very popular.

SHOPPING

Plenty of souvenirs will be offered to you all over Kenya, wherever there is a tourist attraction. Many are distinctly

second rate, and those who want authentic souvenirs should try reputable places where you may well have to pay more. In general, avoid beach hawkers and souvenir stands. You can expect to bargain and may well get reductions, although not always in specialist shops. Most credit cards are accepted in hotel and city shops. There is a small duty free at the airport, offering mostly cigarettes, spirits and souvenirs, but not much variety.

Remember that many animal and reptile products (and, recently, seashells) are prohibited exports, and may be confiscated as imports on return.

Handicrafts: Sculpture is of variable quality and you should shop around. You can find it in several kinds of native woods, and also in soapstone – but this can be very heavy, so consider bulk and weight when buying. Look in the galleries in Nairobi and Mombasa to get an idea of what is available and prices; here you won't be pushed to purchase.

Besides sculpture you can find leather, metalware, curios, weapons, and a vast range of baskets, some beautifully woven in tight, neat patterns. Prices vary enormously and tend to rise in the tourist high season.

Jewellery includes carved stones (loose gems can be purchased), strings of bright beads, earrings, pins of wood and metal. Fabrics can be striking, although in the galleries the best seem to come from countries such as Ghana. There are a lot of batiks. Unusual fabrics, baskets and beadwork can often be found in country markets, so keep your eyes open, compare quality and try to bargain.

Browse in the quality galleries in Nairobi for the best artworks. Such visits also give you an idea of the modern handicrafts which you may find on your travels. Kenya's animal sculptures, for example, are often wooden in both material and execution; you need to look for the genuine artists and not the mere copiers when buying. Quality sculptures and ingenious toys can be found in markets, and the museum shops are good value. Some curio shops are run by self-help societies employing local craftspeople – recommended for fairness and good prices.

Shopping hours vary a great deal, but most shops are open early and close late. In Nairobi, and to a lesser extent in Mombasa, there are many arcades with small, specialist shops.

Markets are open almost every day.

A wall of baskets: Nairobi Market

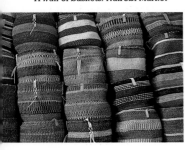

ACCOMMODATION

Hotels

Most people will book direct packages outside Kenya, which provide hotel accommodation as part of the price. However, there is plenty of opportunity for the traveller going alone, or just flying in for a visit. The range, however, is either top class or bargain – there is not a lot in between, especially near the beach resorts or in the game parks. If you don't stay in a lodge, you may be restricted to camping or simple *bandas* – self-catering shelters. Cheaper accommodation at the beaches will normally mean staying in nearby towns and settlements, rather than close to the sea itself. Tourist offices will assist and suggest places to stay, even making bookings for personal visitors. There are also several groupings of hotels, usually based with central telephone numbers in Nairobi. The principal groups are:

African Tours and Hotels, Utalii House, Uhuru Highway, PO Box 30471 (tel: 336858)

Alliance Hotels, College House, University Way, PO Box 46578 (tel: 337501)

Block Hotels, New Stanley House, Standard Street, PO Box 47557 (tel: 335807)

Hilton International, Watalii Street, off Mama Ngina Street, PO Box 30624 (tel: 334000)

Kilimanjaro Club, Grindlays Bank Building, Kenyatta Avenue/Kimathi Street, PO Box 30139 (tel: 582302)

Msafiri Inns, 11th Floor, Utalii House, Uhuru Highway, PO Box 42013 (tel: 229751)

ACCOMMODATION

The imposing Nairobi Hilton

Sarova Hotels, New Stanley Hotel, Kenyatta Avenue, PO Box 30680 (tel: 333248)
Lonrho Lodges and Hotels, Sheikh Karume, Mtango St. (tel: 221047)
Sonotels Kenya, Seventh Floor, Prudential Building, Wabera Street, PO Box 61753 (tel: 227571)

Camping

Camping in Kenya can range from the organised, fully equipped camping safaris to basic tent-pitching in isolated areas. Companies which organise safaris – an attractive option for first-time visitors – range from luxury, individually tailored outfits which will, obviously, be more costly, and will need advance booking such as;

Abercrombie & Kent Ltd, Bruce House, Standard Street, Nairobi (tel: 334955);
to budget safari companies, including the following:
Special Camping Safaris, PO Box 51512, Gilfillan House, Kenyatta Avenue, Nairobi (tel: 338325 or 882541);
Gametrackers, Kenya Cinema, Moi Avenue, Nairobi (tel: 212831 or 330903);
Safari Seekers, Jubilee Insurance Exchange, Kaunda Street, Nairobi (tel: 334585 or 211396);
Safari Camp Services, PO Box 44801, corner of Koinange and Moktar Daddah Streets (tel: 28936 or 330130).
There is a large number and range of campsites in Kenya. The following is a very limited list. Camping in National Parks can generally be arranged via the wardens.
(Also see **Camping** page 114.)

Nairobi
Rowallan Camp, four miles (7km) from city centre, between Kibera and Jamhuri Park. National centre for Kenya's scouts, but also used by tourists. Water, showers, toilets, shop, swimming pool (tel: Warden 568111).
Waterfalls Inn, 19 miles (30km) northwest of city centre, near Limuru. Picnic and Cottage Campsites; riding centre, restaurant and bar, shop, water, toilets, showers.

Mombasa
YWCA, hostel and campsite, 218 yards (200m) uphill from Likoni ferry. Water, toilets, shower. Also a **YMCA**.

Kisumu, Lake Victoria Dunga Restaurant and **Camping**, Hippo Point, two-and-a-half miles (4km) south of town centre. Toilet and sink.
YWCA, hostel and campsite, opposite bus station. Toilet, showers, meals in hostel.

Diani Beach

Dan Trench's, off Diani Beach road. Water, showers, pit toilets. Near shopping centre.

NIGHTLIFE AND ENTERTAINMENT

Nightlife is mostly to be found in the resorts, in central Nairobi, and in Mombasa. There are night clubs in the latter cities, which vary from cheap joints to the quite smart. Popular Nairobi bars include the **Norfolk** terrace, the pub on the first floor of the **Six Eighty Hotel**, and others at principal hotels. There are several discos – note The **New Florida** and **Halliam's Club** in the centre. Others to be found in the surrounding areas such as Eastleigh are noisy, locally popular, and literally jumping.

In Mombasa both main hotels, the **Castle** terrace and the **Manor** bars are crowded at night. There are several clubs in the centre, many of them definitely sleazy, and most around central Moi Avenue. Try Mombasa's **New Florida**, or the busy **Rainbow**. There are plenty more, all indicated with signs.

At beach hotels you are not likely to meet local people, but the entertainments are well run and popular with the hotel's

residents, although not always on every night.

There are concerts at the **Kenya National Theatre**, Moi Avenue, Nairobi; this and the **Donovan Maule Theatre** makes up the city's drama centre.

WEATHER AND WHEN TO GO

This is a country so close to the Equator that all days, throughout the year, are about the same length. You can expect the sun to rise between 06.00 and 06.30hrs, sunset twelve hours on, and of course the sun is almost directly overhead. It also rises and sets rapidly, so the time of dusk is minimal. There is virtually no summer or winter: warm days happen all year round and, as a rule, you are sure of good weather that is rarely uncomfortable.
Temperature and climate vary, however, according to altitude. It can be warm and sometimes humid at the beach, but inland the humidity is less, and as you ascend in height above sea level, it gets even cooler, especially at night. The sunlight is direct and strong (you may need sunglasses and a shady hat) and it can burn without your realising and cause havoc if you are new to it. So take precautions. You can also get dehydrated quite easily; you will probably need to take a supply of bottled water, especially if you are driving or going for a long distance overland.

Wet Periods

Rain is erratic, but usually comes in short showers, and the

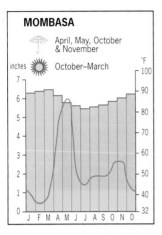

MOMBASA

April, May, October & November

October–March

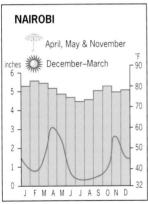

NAIROBI

April, May & November

December–March

sun dries the air rapidly after rain. Whole days of rain are rare. Storms are frequently sharp and violent, often preceded with warning clouds. There are two annual periods of rain, normally expected, though they have come less predictably over recent years – the long and short rains. The former can usually be relied on in the months of April and May, the latter in November and early December. (The dry, hot months come early in the year (January into March), and warm and dry months are June to October.) It can be quite humid just before the rainy periods, which are not necessarily continuous. This can be a good time to visit Kenya, as there will be fewer tourists, since most come in the warm dry periods; consequently, you may find lower prices and easier transport. But remember that Kenya's roads are not solid-surfaced, for the large part, and some marked on maps as perfectly good routes can turn to a wash of mud when it rains, a dustbowl in the heat. You will also find during the rainy periods, however, a seductive country that is refreshingly green and damp.

What To Wear

Depending on where you go, you will probably need fairly light clothes, since much of Kenya is either hot and dry or hot and humid. It may also be cool in the mountains, so plan for that if you are trekking up Mount Kenya; even so remember that the sun is direct and wear headgear and sunglasses. Many people underestimate the strength of the sun and make themselves ill with too much exposure, especially on the beaches, so take care.

For a beach holiday you will probably want to pack evening wear (though not too formal), for dining can be pretty smart affairs at some of the hotels.

HOW TO BE A LOCAL

Kenya is quite an easy-going country and in most parts you will feel quite welcome. It is always as well to remember the colonial past, however. Many Kenyans are very proud of their nation and pleased to be, first and foremost, Kenyans. They are remarkably hospitable and helpful, considering the turbulence of their recent past and their often rough treatment by the land-hungry European and South African settlers of the late 19th and early 20th centuries. (The Kikuyu, in particular, suffered from the dislocation of forced moves from their land, which happened to be some of the most attractive in the country.) An awareness of this can be a considerable help when getting around, and it is wise to learn a few phrases of Swahili, if only to be sociable and polite (see **Language**, page 125). These are not difficult to learn, and their use is a small yet important compliment to the Kenyans on your part. Common courtesy is much appreciated, especially beyond the bounds of Nairobi. A cheery greeting – *jambo* – elicits the same response as a rule, and often a wide smile. Children will respond at once to your interest in how they live and what they enjoy doing. However, there are reports of aggressive behaviour, often from Masai traders. Be polite, yet firm.

Remember that Kenya has a very mixed population – not only Indians, Europeans and residents from neighbouring states, but also many different ethnic groups within the majority black peoples. These tribes can be broken down into large blocks, such as the Kikuyu and the Luo, but there are smaller groupings found all over the country.

Kenya has a number of religions, and some old tribal beliefs still hang on, particularly in rural areas. You can find most Christian sects and a considerable and growing number of Muslims, particularly around Mombasa, and most of the cities will have at least one Indian temple. You are usually free to enter places of worship; however, some mosques are less than welcoming and you may need to request permission.

PERSONAL PRIORITIES

It is much easier to get personal needs in Kenya's cities than in most other African countries, with the exception of South Africa. Soap, washing powders, toiletries (including needs for children), batteries and candles are fairly easily available in the many little supermarkets. Brands may be unfamiliar (home produced or from Third World countries) and often quite cheap.

Supermarkets are often cluttered, and articles difficult to find, but staff will direct you cheerfully. For laundry and dry cleaning you should use the hotel service, if possible – usually cheap and quite good and fast, which it may not be outside.

People used to come to parts of Kenya, particularly places like Malindi, for a sort of sex-fest: not much any more, since the spectre of AIDS. The virus is prevalent in the cities now and many prostitutes are supposed to carry it; in Africa it affects the heterosexual population to a marked degree. Even though sex is often readily available and offered, since Kenya is a fairly free and open society, the best advice is 'don't'; or, if you do, don't fail to use a condom.

Homosexual activity is limited (and illegal), although there is evidence of it in the open life of places like Lamu.

Women travelling alone may experience sexual harassment; avoid empty parts of towns or lonely paths. Some men will attempt the strong come-on, but a resourceful woman can usually handle pests. Be firm and indicate your complete lack of interest.

CHILDREN

Aside from the obvious attraction of the game park animals, the wonderful stretches of soft sand at the Mombasa resorts provide a perfect family holiday. There are swimming pools in most hotels, but much of the sea-bathing is shallow and safe.

The beaches can provide explorations of reef pools, camel rides and opportunities for great picnics. A trip in a glass-bottomed boat, even if children don't snorkel, will enable them to see the engrossing marine life of the Indian Ocean. They will also be able to try aquatic sports or take a trip in an authentic *dhow*.

Near the shore resorts there are many ancient sites to explore, and around them there is usually interesting vegetation with many birds and butterflies to observe (take binoculars as well as cameras). Illustrated books on Kenya's birds, insects and reptiles (not cheap) can be bought at airport and hotel souvenir bookshops. Children should be warned not to feed monkeys, which prowl hotel grounds looking for scraps and can be dangerous, and can give a nasty bite, particularly baboons.

In Nairobi there are attractions such as the **Giraffe Centre** and the orphan-elephants in Langata

Watch but don't touch the intriguing blue or Syke's monkey

(see page 26). There is also the orphan animal enclosure at the **Nairobi National Park**, with afternoon feeding times (see page 30). Also in the Nairobi suburbs are the *Bomas* of Kenya, with regular shows of African dance (see page 26).

Older children will appreciate a visit to one of the Masai villages and a chance to see war dances and spears and shields being made. They will also enjoy camping trips in the game parks, and the most adventurous might enjoy a balloon flight over the animals, but this is expensive. Game drives are a natural attraction, but, unless the child is particularly keen on wildlife, choose parks where there is likely to be plenty to see, such as the Masai-Mara and Amboseli (see pages 41, 80 and 92).

Most restaurants will provide children's meals, and the big towns have fast-food outlets, where snacks, ice-creams and soft drinks are available.

TIGHT BUDGET

Travellers on a budget will find cheaper accommodation can be found away from the centres and beaches, in nearby towns and settlements.

If you are camping, costs will vary according to your style of travel: official campsites charge a fee, but are cheaper than lodgings, which are, in turn, cheaper than hotels.

Organised camping safaris have varying costs, but some can offer bargain trips which are well worth investigating (see under **Accommodation**, page 106, for details). Even those who camp independently will need to set aside money for entry into national parks and reserves. Public transport is relatively cheap – especially the *matatus* (see **Directory**, under **Public Transport**). And cheap snacks can be bought at *hotelis* (restaurants); meals in Nairobi restaurants are much cheaper than the hotels and lodges.

SPECIAL EVENTS

There are very few national events, although local festivities pop up all the time. Agricultural shows take place around the country and have the flavour of a fair.

Islamic events: Ramadhan (March–April); its end a month later is a major event, as is the Prophet's Birthday (September/October).

SPORT

There are stadium buildings in many Kenyan towns, if not a field or patch of land where balls are kicked about.

Football is especially popular. The major clubs play frequent dates (usually Saturdays). New in 1990, Moi International Sports Centre in Ruaraka, is host to the African Games. There is racing at Nairobi's track and each year, during Easter (March/April), a motor rally throughout the country, following a vast loop for four days – the **Safari Rally**.

DIRECTORY

Contents

Arriving

Air

Most visitors to Kenya arrive by air at either of the country's two international airports: Nairobi's Jomo Kenyatta Airport, or Mombasa's Moi International Airport. The country's national carrier, Kenya Airways, operates direct, daily or weekly flights from most European, Asian and African cities, and other major cities of the world. In 1989, it introduced non-stop flights from London (Heathrow) to Nairobi and Mombasa. Around 30 other international airlines fly to Kenya. Most international flights are overnight, arriving in Kenya early in the morning.

The **Jomo Kenyatta Airport**, nine miles (15km) southeast of Nairobi, is one of the most modern and well-equipped in Africa. (A new airport is planned at Eldoret).

Passengers services available include 24-hour currency exchange, cafés, bars, shops, outgoing duty-free shop, tourist information, car rental, first aid and porter services. (Flight information: tel: 822111.)

Transport to the city: Kenya Airways (tel: 433400) provides a 24-hour coach service, approximately every half-hour, journey time 30 minutes. There is a charge for the trip.

There is also public transport (bus number 34) – an hourly service, journey time 45 minutes.

A taxi to the city takes 20 minutes and is a lot more expensive.

Moi International Airport, eight miles (13km) from Mombasa, is the airport most people arrive at on a charter flight. It has 24-hour currency exchange facilities, restaurant, café, bar, outgoing duty-free shop, and car rental desk. (Flight information: tel: 433326.)

Transport: Kenya Airways provides a regular bus service to the city; there is a charge. Taxis are also available at the airport.

DIRECTORY

Road

Kenya has land borders with Tanzania, Uganda, Sudan, Ethiopia and Somalia. All are officially open, but overland travel through southern Sudan and Somalia is inadvisable at present.

Visitors are advised to check the current situation with local embassies/consulates before departing.

Sea

The main entry port is Mombasa; mostly cruise ships. There is, however, a regular passenger service between Mombasa, the Seychelles and Bombay.

Entry Formalities

All visitors must hold a valid passport. Visas are not required by citizens of most Commonwealth countries (exceptions may include Australia and British passport-holders of Indian, Bangladeshi or Pakistani origin) and nationals of certain European countries, including the Republic of Ireland, with whom Kenya has reciprocal waiver arrangements. Americans do need a visa. When a visa is required, application should be made to the nearest Kenyan embassy or consulate 30 days prior to the date of departure. There is now no formal control of how much money you bring in, but it is expected visitors will have sufficient funds for the length of stay, plus return or onward tickets. If these requirements are met, a visitor's pass will be issued, free of charge at your port of entry. This enables you to stay in Kenya for up to three months, extendable (unless there is an objection) from the Immigration Department, Nyayo House, Kenyatta Avenue, PO Box 30191, Nairobi (tel: 332110) or in Mombasa at PO Box 90284 (tel: 311745).

Camping

There are campsites in all game parks and reserves, and it is one of the most exciting ways to have a Kenyan safari. Most camps are serviced, but quality varies enormously from the quite good to the near-invisible. There are also sites around Nairobi and along the coast, while you can camp fairly freely in the country. Surprisingly, there is little danger from wildlife, providing you keep foodstuffs locked away, but you should be aware that there are problems with crime and so you should guard against theft. It is wise to stay near settlements, or even a police station.

If you are at all worried about safety, a camping safari, where you stay in small groups with an experienced guide, is recommended. **Special Camping Safaris Ltd**, Gilfillan House (next to African Heritage), Kenyatta Avenue, PO Box 51512 Nairobi (tel: 338325), offer this service, as do other companies noted under **Accommodation**, page 107.

Chemist see **Pharmacies**.

Crime

Petty (and sometimes violent) crime is a problem in Nairobi and may be encountered in the country, too. It is wise to deposit money and valuables in a hotel

Camping is cheap and enjoyable

safe, and never to carry too much of value, in case of robbery. Tourist centres tend to be crime black-spots. Apart from pickpockets, thieves have an eye for unguarded cases and valuables; never leave possessions unwatched or anything of value in a parked car, whether locked or not. It is sensible to leave cars in guarded lots. (You will notice many private guards or *askaris* on city streets at night.) Be careful of valuables on crowded city streets, and transport, and it is unwise to walk alone after dark. Some game parks can be distinctly dangerous for campers, and can be the scene for muggings. Even places like the Nyong Hills are not safe, by night or day.

Customs Regulations

There are specific allowances of alcohol, cigarettes and luxury goods. Duty free allowance for those over 16 years of age on entering the country: 200 cigarettes or 50 cigars or up to 250 grams (8.825 ounces) of

tobacco or tobacco products; one litre bottle of spirits or wine and 0.5 litre (0.88 pint) of toilet water and perfume of which not more than 0.125 litre (0.22 pint) may be perfume. A reasonable amount of personal effects, including still cameras, unlimited film, and binoculars may be freely imported; however, be prepared to provide refundable deposits for the temporary importation of radios, tape-recorders, and video equipment. Gifts will be charged duty. You are not allowed to bring into the country agricultural produce or pets. Firearms may only be imported with a certificate.
Currency: There is a limit on the amount of import or export of Kenyan currency, but no insistence any longer on a minimum sum in convertible currency to be brought in. Your currency 'balance' may be checked on your departure. On departure you will be required

to exchange excess Kenyan currency you still hold at a bank or exchange point (banks at the two international airports maintain a 24-hour service).

Departure

There is a departure tax of $20 US, or equivalent, per person on leaving from Kenya's airports. Remaining Kenyan currency should be converted to a foreign currency before departure – always possible, as banks at the airports are open 24 hours. It is a good idea to keep a few small Kenyan notes to buy refreshments while waiting for departure. There is also a domestic airport tax of 50 Kenyan cents. Most flight departures are at night. You are advised to arrive at least two hours before take-off, to allow time for the above procedures.

Crossing into neighbouring countries: You can cross the border, but check that you have all the necessary papers and inoculations if you plan to visit Tanzania, Uganda, Sudan, Ethiopia or Somalia. You should contact the appropriate country's diplomatic mission in Kenya. You are most likely to go to Tanzania, represented in Nairobi at Continental House (fourth floor), corner of Harambee Avenue and Uhuru Highway, PO Box 47790 (tel: 331150).

Driving

There is a nationwide speed limit of 62mph (100kph); 31mph (50kph) in cities; and 18½ mph (30kph) in game parks and reserves.

Driving is on the left. Lighting up time is officially 18.30hrs and seat belts must be worn at all times.

Driving is not of good standard, and roads are often badly surfaced with holes; some of the better ones have 'sleeping policemen', or humps, to slow the traffic.

Principal roads are in general good, but away from the main areas they can get rough – very rough indeed on the dirt (*murram*) roads in the northern areas, where four-wheel drive vehicles are often employed and travelling can be hard. In the rainy periods some small roads can get washed out or become boggy; alternatively they can get very dusty in dry weather.

Nairobi suffers from too much traffic and extended rush hours, and during the weekdays parking is a problem, although not outside the capital. Be careful of lorries and *matatus* (buses): they often drive fast and erratically. Pull over and stop if sirens sound and headlights shine for the President's cars.

Fuel contains ethanol, which can cause problems in hot weather. It is measured in litres. Premium grade is used in the majority of cars.

Documents: your own driving licence is valid after endorsement at the Road Transport Office, or take an international driving licence.

Car Hire: to hire a car you must be over 23 and under 70 years of age and have held a driving licence for a minimum of two years. It is a good idea to take your passport along as well.

There are many small firms offering both self- and chauffeur-driven cars. If in doubt there are branches of the generally dependable **Avis** and **Hertz** in town centres and at airports. Hertz reservations: tel: 331960 (Nairobi), and 316333 (Mombasa). Shop around for the best value – prices tend to be high. Check your vehicle thoroughly before attempting a long-distance drive.

Breakdown: most reputable car hire firms are members of the Automobile Association of Kenya (AAK), who have patrols on the major highways, while in the parks nearly all lodges have resident mechanics. In the event of a breakdown phone the car rental company, who will deal with the situation.

Prior to departure it is a good idea to contact the AAK at Nyaku House, Hurlingham, PO Box 40087, Nairobi (tel: 720382), for up-to-date information on road conditions and other touring-related matters. Always carry some spare fuel and water.

Electricity

The supply is 240 volts, 50 cycles AC. Most sockets are square, three-pin. Generally a 110-volt razor point is also available.

If required, most major hotels and lodges will be able to provide adaptors for 110 volts, 60 cycles.

Embassies

Kenyan Embassies Abroad

Australia: visitors should refer to the British Embassy in Canberra

Canada: Gillin Building, Suite 600, 141 Laurier Avenue, West Ottawa, Ontario KIP 5J3 (tel: (616) 563-1773)

UK: Kenya House, 45 Portland Place, London W1Y 9HD (tel: 0171-636 2371)

US: 2249 R Street NW, Washington DC 20008 (tel: (202) 387-6101)

Embassies in Kenya

Australia: Development House (third floor), Moi Avenue, PO Box 30360, Nairobi (tel: 334666)

Canada: Comcraft House (sixth floor), Haile Selassie Avenue, Nairobi (tel: 214804)

UK: Bruce House (third, 12th, 13th and 14th floors), Standard Street, Nairobi (tel: 335944)

US: US Embassy Building, Norfolk Towers, Kijake Street, PO Box 30137, Nairobi (tel: 442567 or 222166)

Emergency Telephone Numbers

From direct dial telephones, dial 999 for police, fire and ambulance services, or go through the operator in rural areas where they will have special local numbers. Check the pink pages in the phone book.

For the Flying Doctor (see also **Health Regulations**) dial 501301 in Nairobi.

Entertainment Information

Several large cinemas can be found in central Nairobi and in Mombasa showing American, British and European films. There are concerts at the National Theatre from time to time, and recitals at the British Council auditorium in Nairobi.

DIRECTORY

For African culture try the *Bomas* of Kenya shows every afternoon, outside central Nairobi (see page 26). The International Casino in Nairobi has the most sophisticated entertainment.

Entry Formalities see Arriving

Health Regulations

Although the official leaflets suggest you only need to protect yourself against malaria, which is endemic in many areas outside Nairobi and the highlands, especially in the hot and humid areas around the coast and in the bush, it is suggested that you also have protection for other infections. Malaria may need two sets of tablets, weekly and daily, although it is claimed that the daily dose should suffice by some doctors – check with your GP. You will need a course starting at least two weeks before you leave for Africa and continued for at least two more weeks after your return; Malaria prophylactics are available without prescription from chemists or drugstores. Inoculation against yellow fever and cholera, though not mandatory for European, American and Australian visitors, is advised. Visitors arriving from yellow fever- or cholera-infected areas should, however, carry inoculation certificates. Immunisation against typhoid, polio, tetanus and, due to recent infections, meningitis are also worth considering. Also recommended is gamma globulin, against hepatitis A. It is essential you check the current situation, before you leave, with your nearest Kenya Tourist Office, diplomatic mission, or travel agent. You can

Dancers from the Bomas *of Kenya*

obtain injections via your own GP, but allow time for this. Should you require medical assistance while you are away, both Nairobi and Mombasa have highly qualified doctors, surgeons, and dentists whom your hotel can contact for you; other main towns also have good hospital care. Most travel agents and tour operators subscribe to the Flying Doctor Service, but if you are not going through one of these, then get temporary membership, lasting for one month. Membership entitles you to free air transport from anywhere in Kenya to a medical centre. Contact: **The Flying Doctor Service**, PO Box 30125, Nairobi (tel: 501301).

If you should fall ill after arriving home, never forget to tell your doctor that you have been in a country where malaria can be contracted. It is easily treated, but if not suspected can appear to be something else, and the wrong treatment can cause dangerous delays.

It is safe to swim in the sea and swimming pools, but swimming in freshwater lakes and rivers should be avoided, as there is a danger of waterborne infections such as that inflicted by the Bilharzia parasite.

Drinking local water can cause acute stomach problems, and some foods can also be difficult. Always use bottled water and, if your stomach is delicate, eat carefully and do not touch uncooked produce.

Note: AIDS is a major problem in Africa and it is widespread among heterosexuals in Kenya. Any form of sexual activity is therefore fraught with the possibility of contact.

Holidays
The following dates are national holidays, when most businesses, banks, shops and services close:
1 January – New Year's Day
March/April – Good Friday and Easter Monday
1 May – Labour Day
1 June – Madaraka Day (commemorating Kenya's attainment of self-government)
10 October – Moi Day (commemorating President Moi's installation)
20 October – Kenyatta Day (commemorating the arrest of the first president of Kenya in 1952)
12 December – Independence Day
25 December – Christmas Day
26 December – Boxing Day
The Muslim festival of *Idd-ul-Fitr* is also a public holiday, the date varying according to the Ramadhan season.

Lost Property
Most people are honest, but if you leave something it may be assumed you intended to do so and kept. Some hotels maintain lost property offices. If you give items to staff, you should sign a chit indicating your permission.

Media
Kenya has several English-language newspapers. Publications include the *Daily Nation*, *Kenya Times*, *Standard* and a news magazine, the *Weekly Review*. Foreign papers are available at major

hotels and news-stands, a day or so late. The free, tourist-aimed *Coast Week* gives news, sports and entertainment information. It concentrates on Kenya, but includes Tanzania and the Seychelles.
Tourist's Kenya is a free publication with information on nearly everything for the visitor to Kenya – game parks, safaris, accommodation, restaurants, entertainment, sports, shopping, maps etc. It is available from hotels and tourist offices.
Kenya has a number of English-language radio stations and the BBC World Service can be picked up on the following frequencies (KHz – Kilohertz):
Morning   15420   7160   6155
Daytime   21470   17885   15420
Evening   15420   15070   9140

Money Matters
Kenya's currency is based upon the decimal system. The unit is the Kenya Shilling (KES or Shs), divided into 100 cents (cts). Coins: 5 and 10 cents (bronze) and 50 cents, 1 and 5 shillings (silver). Notes: 10, 20, 50, 100, 200 and 500 shillings and a 1000 shilling note has just been introduced.
In transactions you may sometimes hear 20 shillings referred to as a 'pound', and the 20 shillings note called a 'pound note'. It is an offence to damage or deface Kenyan currency. Travellers' cheques are universally accepted. Credit cards are almost universally accepted in principal shops, hotels, lodges, restaurants and services. American Express, Visa and Master Card, Merchant, Royal, Eurocard and Senator are the most often seen; some places will only take one. Credit cards are not accepted in Tanzania. You *must* change foreign currency only at banks or hotels licensed for foreign exchange. You may be asked to show what money you have, as a check that you are not leaving with Kenyan money, or that you have not changed currency on the black markets (see also **Arriving** and **Departure**).
All major towns have banks with a *Bureau de Change* open every weekday from 09.00 to 14.00hrs, and also in the mornings on the first and last Saturdays of the month from 09.00 to 11.00hrs, excluding national holidays. Banks in Nairobi, Mombasa and Malindi open until 16.30 or 17.00hrs Monday to Saturday (sometimes closing lunchtimes on Saturdays). Airport banks are open 24 hours, so if in doubt use them. Principal banks are Barclays Bank of Kenya, Kenya Commercial Bank, Standard Bank, National Bank of Kenya and Commercial Bank of Africa.

Opening Times
Offices: 08.00–13.00 and 14.00–17.00hrs, Monday to Friday.
Shops: 08.30–12.30 and 14.00–16.30hrs, Monday to Saturday.
Banks: see **Money Matters**
Post Offices: see **Post Office**
National Museums: 09.30–18.00hrs daily.

Personal Safety see **Crime** and **Health Regulations**

Nairobi Mosque's perfect symmetry

Pharmacies
There are chemists dispensing prescription and over the counter treatments in all major centres. Try **Elton's** on Aga Khan Walk in Nairobi, open every weekday (tel: 339099). In Mombasa try **London Pharmacy Ltd**, Motor Mart Building, Moi Avenue (tel: 25885).
Visitors requiring special and continued medication should bring sufficient to cover the duration of their stay.

Places of Worship
Most Kenyans are Christians or Muslims and there are places of worship in most major cities, and at least one Indian temple.

Police
Kenya's police force is renowned for its efficiency (in an emergency dial 999).
Visitors are advised to observe the laws in the case of Foreign Exchange Control, traffic regulations, prostitution, sexual abuse and taking or trafficking in drugs. Offenders are dealt with seriously.

Post Office
Post offices are open 08.00–17.00hrs Monday to Friday and 08.00–13.00hrs Saturday. Most hotels also operate a postal service for their guests.

Public Transport
Air
Kenya Airways operates an extensive network of internal flights, which includes scheduled services from Nairobi to Mombasa, Malindi, Lamu Island and Kisumu, as well as inclusive tours to the game parks and the coast. For reservations (Nairobi) tel: (02) 332750 or 822111.
There are also private airlines which operate light aircraft to small air strips. Major companies include Africair, Air Kenya, Caspair, Pioneer,

Prestige Air and Sunbird. They operate from Nairobi's Wilson Airport. Sunbird operates regular flights to the Masai-Mara and Lamu.

Rail
Kenya Railways operates a fairly modern, if somewhat limited service.
The only routes are:
Nairobi–Mombasa;
Nairobi–Kisumu;
Nairobi–Malaba;
Voi–Taveta (in the southeastern corner of the country).
Travel is in de luxe, second or third class carriages. All upper class places are normally booked in advance; overseas travellers may reserve up to three months in advance. The most likely route to be travelled is the Nairobi–

Matatus, Kenya's buses, are an experience in themselves

Mombasa connection, which leaves every night (two services) and takes about 14 hours. You will need to book and, in second class, pay for bedding, but it is still a bargain, with a really old-style dining car and pleasant, concerned service. The trains leave twice a day (evenings) from Nairobi and Mombasa.

Bus
In Kenya this is almost entirely by the small, busy, brightly painted little Nissan-type *matatus*, which are, in fact, privately-owned vans, so you need either to bargain or ask the cost of a journey when you get on. At Nairobi's stations the drivers tout for custom, advertising where they are going and how much it will be. The bus will usually be crowded, the going sometimes rough, but it is a

good way to see the real Kenya.

On some major roads, such as the busy but very pot-holed Mombasa–Nairobi highway, you can take bigger and speedier bus transport. It is cheap, and has the advantage of getting you (on a good level road) much more directly to your destination, since the *matatus* may make detours to drop or pick up, and they do make frequent stops. They are however, a bargain.

Many large hotels offer their own bus services, which may be less crowded and cleaner, but are also correspondingly more expensive.

Taxis

Not hailed, but there are taxi ranks, usually outside hotels and central points. They are available at many areas in Nairobi and Mombasa and at rail and bus stations. They will usually find you, with drivers loudly accosting you for trade and offering services. Ask, before you get in, how much a journey will be. There can be extra charges for numbers and luggage. The cars can sometimes be ancient and wheezy, but they get around and drivers are friendly, and it is always wise to take a taxi to a part of town unknown to you, especially after dark. (London-type taxis are available too).

Ferries

These run between Mombasa, Malindi and Lamu. Contact the local tourist office and tour operators for schedules.

Telephones

There is a fairly good service within the country, but there are not too many telephones. The entire country has only three telephone books! Payphones, often awkward to operate, take KES 3 for local calls.

Most major Kenyan towns are covered by the direct-dial system.

The code for Nairobi is 02. Other area codes in Kenya include:

Athi River	0150
Diani Beach	01261
Eldoret	0321
Embu	0161
Kakamega	0331
Kericho	0361
Kisumu	035
Malindi	0123
Meru	0164
Mombasa	011
Nakuru	037
Nanyuki	017
Nyeri	0171
Thika	0151

For enquiries dial 991.

For the local operator dial 900.

The speaking clock is 993.

For calls outside Kenya you can dial direct for most countries. To make a call dial the international access code; next the country code (for the UK 44; Eire 353; US and Canada 1; Australia 61; New Zealand 64); followed by the area code, minus the initial '0'; and finally, the subscriber's number.

If you encounter any difficulty, check with the international operator – the number is 0195.

Time

Local time is Greenwich Mean

DIRECTORY

Time plus three hours. Nairobi and the rest of Kenya is three hours ahead of London; eight hours ahead of New York and Montreal; 11 hours ahead of San Francisco and Vancouver; seven hours behind Sydney; and nine hours behind New Zealand. Sunrise is between 05.45 and 06.15hrs; sundown is from 18.30 to 19.00hrs. Kenya follows the Christian calendar.

Tipping

Most hotels, lodges, tented camps and restaurants include a service charge of around 10 per cent, but if you are particularly pleased with service a small additional sum is appreciated. It is customary to tip for bar service, around 10 per cent. Tour drivers also expect a small tip, though again you should only give if satisfied with the service.

It is sensible to keep a supply of coins, although the fact that you have notes in very low denominations is useful.

Toilets

There are quite a few public toilets, but they are often filthy. Try big hotels, restaurants, or ask while visiting the larger shops.

Tourist Offices

In Kenya tourist offices are set up in most centres and give free advice and accommodation information, as well as making bookings. In the large cities the staff are helpful, and will do all they can to assist you. With tours arranged through government tourist offices, you are fairly sure of a satisfactory arrangement.

Unfortunately, agencies offering private tours are not always dependable.

The main tourist office in Kenya is located at:

Utalii House, off Uhuru Highway, PO Box 30027, Nairobi (tel: (02) 331030); or opposite the Hilton Hotel.

Travel Agencies

There are a great many tour operators offering tours and safaris throughout Kenya. Many operators have offices in Nairobi.

Some established companies include:

Kenya Wildlife Trails
Kimathi House
(opposite the New Stanley Hotel)
PO Box 44687
Nairobi
(tel: (02) 228960)

Keytours
Reinsurance Plaza
Taifa Road
PO Box 19580
Nairobi
(tel: (02) 331815)

Safari World
Nairobi Hilton
Watalii Street
PO Box 56803
(tel: (02) 336242)

United Touring Group
Fedha Towers
(corner of Muindi Mbingu and Kaunda Streets)
PO Box 42196
Nairobi
(tel: (02) 331960)

Universal Safari Tours
Cotts House (ground floor)
City Hall Way
PO Box 49313
Nairobi
(tel: (02) 221446)

LANGUAGE

In common with many other African states, Kenya has a number of tribal tongues. There are however, only three main language groups in Africa, and they provide the root for the many tribal variations. These are Bantu, Hamitic and Nilotic. There are examples of these throughout Kenya.

Although you may be interested in hearing these varied tongues, it is only Swahili that you will need, other than English, which is extensively understood in the cities. Ki-Swahili is understood by most East Africans today, along with their own tribal tongue. It's not difficult to learn a few words, and pronunciation is easy as every letter is sounded fully except ch and sh, which are as in English.

Kenyans are usually quite pleased to help out.

hello habari (*jambo* is often used to/by tourists)
goodbye kwaheri
thank you asante
I'm fine nzuri
please tafadhali
what is your name? jina lako nani?
my name is... jina langu ni...
yes ndiyo
no hapana
fine haya
I want to go to ... mimi nataka kwenda...
left kwa kushoto
right kwa kulia
straight moja kwa moja
food chakula

water maji
vegetables mboga
fruit matunda
fish samaki
meat nyama
chicken kuku
coffee kahawa
tea chai
fruit juice maji ya tamu
how much is this? hii bei gani?
fixed price bei moja
doctor daktari
hospital hospitali
day siku
daytime mchana
night-time usiku
week wiki
month mwezi
year mwaka

Days
Monday jumatatu
Tuesday jumanne
Wednesday jumatano
Thursday alhamisi
Friday ijumaa
Saturday jumamosi
Sunday jumapili

Numbers
one moja
two mbili
three tatu
four ine
five tano
six sita
seven saba
eight nane
nine tisa
10 kumi
20 ishirini
30 thelathini
40 arobaini
50 hamsini
60 sitini
70 sabini
80 themanini
90 tisini
100 mia

INDEX/ACKNOWLEDGEMENTS

The Automobile Association would like to thank the following
photographers and libraries for their assistance in the preparation of
this book:

ERIC MEACHER took all the photographs (© AA Photo Library) except:

NATURE PHOTOGRAPHERS LTD 6 Mount Kenya (D Hutton), 9 Gedi (A J
Cleave), 11 Impala, 12 Samburu National Park (M E Gore), 30 Ostrich
(H Miles), 31 Aberdare Highlands (M E Gore), 32 Speckled mousebird
(R S Daniel), 34 Mount Kenya (M E Gore), 40 Leopard (H Miles), 59
Sand dunes, Malindi, 60 Waterholes, Tsavo National Park (A J Cleave),
62 Crab plover (R S Daniel), 63 Mangrove swamp (A J Cleave), 68
Cinnamon-chested bee-eater (R S Daniel), 71 Rift Valley (A J Cleave),
72/3 Lake Nakuru (P R Sterry), 74 Black rhinos (H Van Lawick), 75
Skimmer (J F Reynolds), 77 Abyssinian roller (E A Janes), 79 Lions (H
Van Lawick), 86 Lake Magadi (P Davey), 91 Hell's Gate (D Hutton), 92
Spotted hyaena (M E Gore), 95 Grant's gazelle (H Van Lawick), 96
Samburu National Park (E A Janes), 99 Zebra and wildebeest (P R
Sterry), 103 Secretary bird (J F Reynolds), 111 Blue monkey (M E
Gore).

SPECTRUM COLOUR LIBRARY Cover: Kilimanjaro.

Author's Acknowledgements

The author would like to thank Tropical Places (Travel), Forest Row,
Sussex; Patrick Orr of Raitt-Orr PR; and Genevieve McCourt of
Tamarind for their help in the original preparation of Essential Kenya.

Contributors
For this revision:
Copy editor: Sheila Hawkins
Thanks also to **Michael Leech**, the **Kenya National Tourist Office** (London)
and the **AAK** (Automobile Association of Kenya) for their assistance.